CHILI!

Mouth-Watering Meatless Recipes

ROBERT OSER

Book Publishing Company
Summertown, Tennessee

All rights reserved. Published in the United States by
The Book Publishing Company
P.O. Box 99
Summertown, TN 38483
1-888-260-8458

Cover painting: Kim Trainor

Cover design: Christa Schoenbrodt

Interior design: Warren C. Jefferson

1-57067-070-6

Oser, Robert
        Chili! : mouth-watering meatless recipes / Robert Oser.
                p.   cm.
        Includes index.
        ISBN 1-57067-070-6 (alk. paper)
        1. Chili 2. Vegetarian cookery 3. Cookery, American.
        I. Title.
        TX749.084   1999
        641.8'23--dc21   98-51404
                                                CIP

04 03 02 01 00 99   1 2 3 4 5 6 7 8 9

TABLE OF CONTENTS

Introduction • 8
Chile Heat • 26
How to Use Chiles • 21
Bean Basics • 28
Notes on the Ingredients • 37
Glossary • 46

Basic Chilis • 49

Traditional Chilis • 59
Native American
Mexican & Southwestern

Chilis with a Slight Twist • 77

Chilis with a Big Twist • 93

Chilis Around the World • 105

Nuclear Meltdown Chili • 120

Ingredient Sources • 122
Index • 125

CHILI!

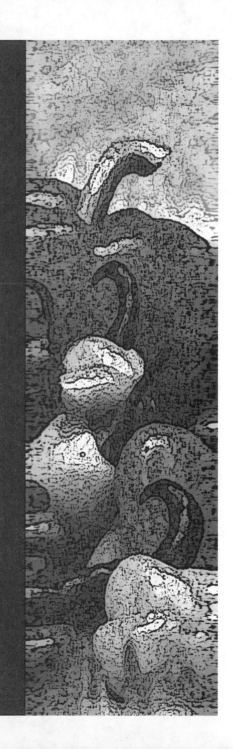

Introduction • 8

Chile Heat • 26

How to Use Chiles •21

Bean Basics • 28

Notes on the Ingredients • 37

Glossary • 46

Introduction—Of Chilis and Chiles

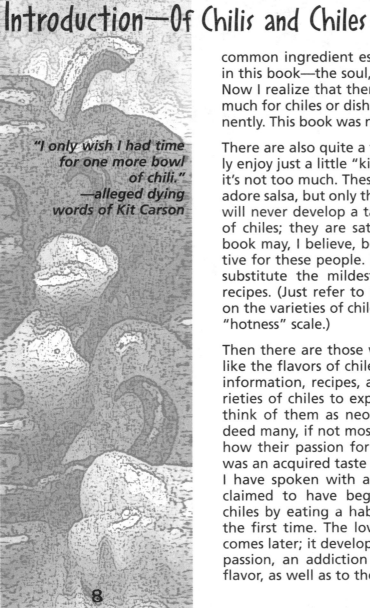

"I only wish I had time for one more bowl of chili."
—alleged dying words of Kit Carson

8

Okay, let's begin right at the heart of the matter. Chile peppers are the common ingredient essential to all of the recipes in this book—the soul, if you will, of these dishes. Now I realize that there are those who don't care much for chiles or dishes that feature them prominently. This book was not written for these people.

There are also quite a few people who occasionally enjoy just a little "kick" to their food, as long as it's not too much. These are the people who really adore salsa, but only the mild variety. Perhaps they will never develop a taste for the hotter varieties of chiles; they are satisfied where they are. This book may, I believe, be very helpful and informative for these people. However, they may need to substitute the mildest forms of chiles in these recipes. (Just refer to pages 16-20 for the section on the varieties of chiles and where they fit on the "hotness" scale.)

Then there are those who have found they really like the flavors of chiles and are looking for more information, recipes, and, especially, different varieties of chiles to experience and enjoy. I like to think of them as neophyte chile aficionados. Indeed many, if not most, "fire-eaters" like to recall how their passion for the more incendiary chiles was an acquired taste that evolved slowly. No one I have spoken with about hot peppers has ever claimed to have begun their relationship with chiles by eating a habañero, or even a jalapeño, the first time. The love of the "caustic" peppers comes later; it develops, evolves, and grows into a passion, an addiction to the fiery sensation and flavor, as well as to the experience itself.

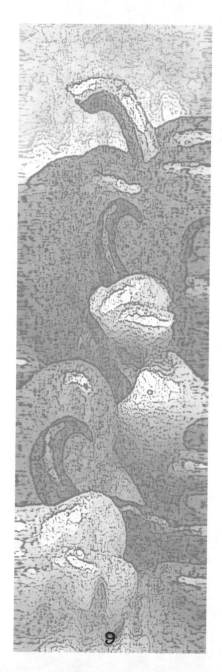

Although it's likely not politically correct to compare the chile experience with the experience of someone getting "high" on a drug for the first time, there are many passionate chile fans who describe their experiences in just such a way. Later, we'll discuss the scientific reasons for the connection. The noted physician/author/lecturer—and chile-lover—Andrew Weil, in his book, *Marriage of the Sun and Moon,* describes it this way:

> *"A person uninitiated into the mysteries of chili-eating who bites down on a really peppy capsicum pod, may exhibit all the symptoms of furious rabies. It is difficult to convey to such a sufferer the truth that relief comes only of eating more chilies, but that is the case . . . Here we separate the chili lovers from the chili haters. There are those who believe that cayenne pepper is to be dispensed in barely visible pinches and Tabasco sauce in minuscule drops. I am not one of them. To me, chilies are an inviting challenge, and I strive to master the art of eating them like a true son of the Americas. I have watched Mexicans cover a slice of fresh pineapple with powdered red chili. I have seen them eat whole pickled jalapeños between bites of sandwiches and cover tortillas with smoky, barbecued chipotle peppers, so hot you expect them to eat through their containers. I have seen Mexican youths engage in chili-eating contests to extend their limits. I can tell by their expressions that all of these people are onto something good."*

This book is intended especially for that fraternity (or sorority, if you prefer) of chile "addicts." They may be hard to spot in the general congregation. After all, they don't wear special uniforms or buttons that declare their allegiance to the capsicum.

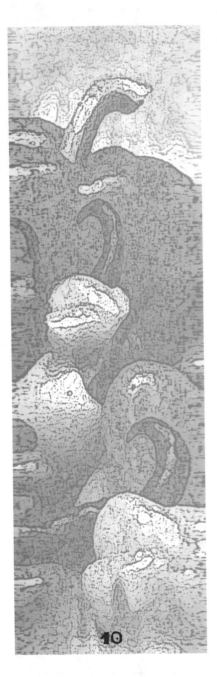

But, like addicts everywhere, one can generally spot another. There are telltale signs that eventually give us away. Perhaps it's the bottle of Tabasco nestled with the salt and pepper on the table, always within arm's reach. Or it may be the way the pepperoncinis are the first item to disappear from the antipasto platter at the Italian restaurant. If the waiter at the Indian restaurant asks your dining companion if they would like their order mild or hot and they answer, "very hot . . . and could you bring some chili paste on the side?"—you know you have someone else on your chile wavelength.

If you are reading this introduction, you may well be one of us. If your mouth salivates at the thought of a spicy curry, a fiery Szechwan dish, or a plate of enchiladas smothered in salsa, these recipes may be just what you're looking for: full of tasty ingredients, simple enough to be almost foolproof, and at the same time, open for change and creativity—the personal touch.

At the end of each of my recipes, I always end with "Enjoy!" I was explaining to my beautiful partner, Donna, that I hoped to give everyone a subliminal message. "Subliminal?" she answered. "There's nothing subliminal about that message. It's out front in everything you do."

Well, I have to admit she's got me pegged. Cooking, eating, sharing, all that we do, all that we are is meant to be enjoyed. If you enjoy these recipes or ideas, please let me know. Feel free, always, to change these recipes in any way that pleases you. You will never hurt my feelings by personalizing these recipes to fit your tastes and needs. Recipes are suggestions. These worked for me at one time or another, but as I'm the type of cook who seldom makes a recipe the same way twice, I will probably change a few ingredients the next time I make these recipes, depending on my mood, what I have on hand, what's available at the market, or who I am making the dish for.

Chilis or Chiles?

What is, then, the correct spelling? You will see both of these spellings used, as well as chilli, chillie, chilie, and a few others in many books, articles, and recipes. I would hesitate to say what is the correct or incorrect spelling. (In Spanish, it seems "chile" is the correct term and the spelling "chili" is an Americanized version.) Anyway, I have my ideas and preferences, and it seems that I'm right in line with many other cooks/authors in making the following generalized rule. At least in this book, I will use the spelling "chile" to refer to the chile pepper itself, and "chili" to refer to the stew or dish for which the "chile" is an ingredient.

Chiles throughout History

The term "pepper" applied to chiles is actually a misnomer. One of the main purposes for Columbus' journey, during which he "discovered" the New World, was to find a shorter route to the Orient, the source of spices and seasonings increasingly in demand throughout the Old World. One of the more popular spices that Columbus was looking for was black pepper. Although he didn't find black pepper on that voyage, he did discover plants whose fruits were more pungent than anything yet known to cooks in Europe, and they became known as peppers.

CHILIS!

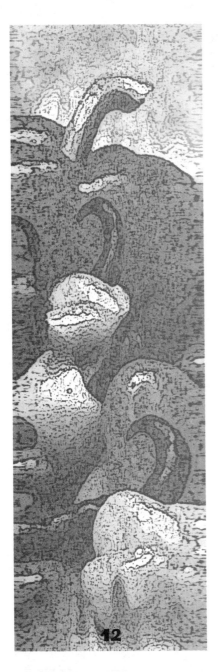

Though chiles were common ingredients in Native American cooking, they were also strung together on strings and hung on canoes and in dwellings for good luck. They were considered so important to several indigenous cultures that they were used for trade, as well as a form of currency. But mainly, of course, they were good to eat, adding a very desirable flavor to previously bland dishes.

Actually, according to one estimate, more than 60% of the plants and grains now eaten in the world today originated in the Americas and are of Indian origin. No matter what else Columbus may be thanked or blamed for, this discovery was the start of many important ethnic and cultural cuisines. Where, after all, would Italian cuisine be without the tomato or Irish cooking be without the potato, both indigenous to the Americas?

Technically chiles are a member of the genus Capsicum, related to nightshades such as tomatoes, potatoes, and eggplant. All capsicums start as green fruit and, when ripened, become various shades of red, yellow, or orange. Green and red bell peppers, for instance, are sweet, very mild varieties of capsicum, the green being the unripened form of the fruit. (Botanically, capsicum, having seeds, is classified as fruit like tomatoes and cucumbers, though all three are generally known as and used in culinary circles as vegetables.) Hotter varieties of capsicum are generally known as chile peppers or chiles.

After Columbus's discovery, chiles were cultivated so quickly and established themselves so well to the climate and cultures of Africa, Southeast Asia, and India that they were often thought to have been native to those lands. Today you cannot think of the cuisine of, say, Thailand, India, or

Ethiopia, without gratitude for the role that chiles have played in spicing up these wonderful dishes.

Evidence exists that New World Indians were probably enjoying wild chiles around 8,000 years ago and began cultivating them about 5,000 years ago. With the spread of chile cultivation to Asia, India, and Africa, chiles gained popularity throughout tropical and temperate climates all over the world. Even cuisines that shy from the hotter varieties of chiles often incorporate milder chiles and peppers, such as bell peppers, Hungarian wax peppers, banana peppers, etc.

Part of the reason for the popularity of chiles is that they help the body adjust to climate and weather. Chiles tend to warm the body in cooler weather and cool the body in warmer weather. Although many gringos tend to avoid chiles in warmer months, natives of tropical climates enjoy chiles' cooling effects throughout the hot spells.

It's always interesting to me when discussing chile peppers with the inexpe- ## To your health!

rienced to watch people shrink back as if repulsed. You know that they're thinking, "Something that hot can't be good for you."

In reality, chiles are an important and very healthful part of the diet of many cultures around the world, and many medicinal benefits have been attributed to them, with more being discovered all the time.

To begin with, chile peppers are one of the richer sources of vitamin C, even more so than citrus fruits. They are also a pretty good source of vitamin A (as beta carotene) and a few minerals, in-

13

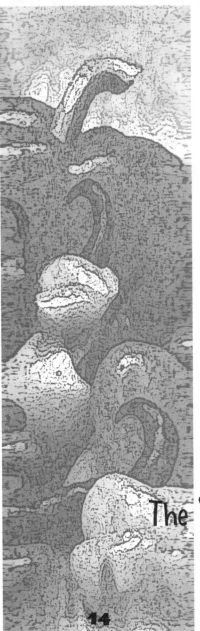

cluding calcium and phosphorus. (By the way, when peppers are dried, they lose most of their C content but their Vitamin A content is increased 100 times.)

Although the irritation that accompanies the eating of chiles can be quite intense, it does not seem to do any damage to the body. (It only feels that way.) In reality, capsicum has long been known as beneficial for the stomach and digestive processes. In fact, contrary to what many may think, red pepper has long been used for the treatment of ulcers and gastritis. It is also said to be an effective blood purifier and can be helpful in clearing the respiratory tract. Some studies have shown capsicum to work as an anticoagulant, possibly helping prevent heart attacks or strokes caused by blood clots.

Applied in poultices or as a plaster, red pepper relieves muscle pain and rheumatism. Although the sensation may be quite intense, red pepper is often added to open sores and wounds to help them heal quickly. Oil of capsicum may be helpful topically in relieving toothache pain.

Studies are being done on red peppers in the treatment of the symptoms of PMS. It will certainly be interesting to see what other beneficial uses of capsicum are yet to be discovered.

The "High" of Chiles

Yes, chiles do add a wonderful flavor to many dishes and, yes, they are also a healthful part of the diet, but the passion many feel for this humble fruit lies even beyond this. When hot chiles are ingested, the sensation is immediate and quite intense. The eater feels a burning that spreads throughout the body. The nose begins to run, the eyes begin to tear, pain in the mouth and throat becomes so intense as to be almost unbearable, and the body begins to perspire freely. As a response to the intense sensation caused by the peppers, the body releases endorphins, a sort of natural painkiller (similar in some aspects to morphine). The intense bodily reactions to chiles are similar to the euphoria felt by athletes after strenuous performance, and it is this "rush" that the chile lover soon learns to enjoy—and seek. Having enjoyed both chile peppers and running for many years, I can readily identify with those who describe the rush of eating hot chiles as feeling like a "runner's high."

Why is it, then, that others can have the same experience, the endorphin rush and all, and notice only the "pain" of the experience? Chile lovers and chile haters, it seems, both experience the same sensations, yet one group sees it as a negative, painful experience and the other, while conscious of the pain, can't wait to experience the sensation again in more powerful doses! Ah, but human differences are one of the mysteries that makes us so marvelous and interesting. I know many who swear by beer and yet, though I occasionally enjoy the flavor of a good imported or micro-brewed bottled beer, I find I always stop at one because I simply do not enjoy the "buzz" that drinking more than one beer gives me. C'est la vie.

But if you are one who does enjoy the sensation of "setting yourself afire from the inside" by eating hot chiles, even if still a novice at "the art of fire-eating," know that it is often a learned process. Many aficionados start with milder peppers and experiment with different varieties in varying amounts and in blends with other chiles and spices, finding flavors they prefer and heat levels

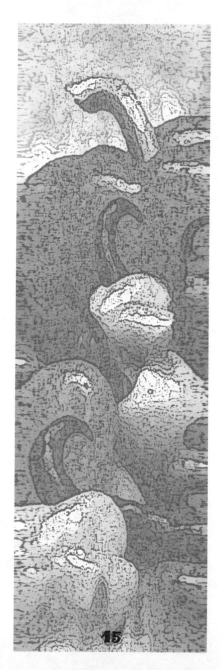

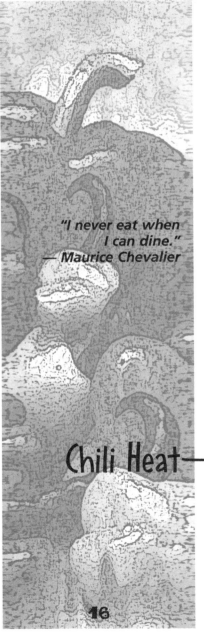

"I never eat when I can dine."
— *Maurice Chevalier*

they can tolerate. As their tolerance builds, they move up to yet stronger varieties of capsicum, say cayenne or serrano peppers. Eventually they find the lure of the ultimate peppers—Thai, Scotch bonnets, and habañeros—irresistible.

At first, for some chile addicts, it becomes almost a contest, a "macho" test to see who can withstand the most pain. However, for those who truly appreciate the subtle beauty of the "chile high," it's not so much the intensity of the sensation that counts but the harmony of flavors and sensations being enjoyed by those in the throes of a "chile experience." In other words, I've learned to enjoy using very small amounts of several different varieties of chiles (and other seasonings), adjusting the amounts according to not only heat but sweetness, smokiness, dried or fresh, etc., to match my mood as both cook and diner. But, then, perhaps I'm just growing older. (Wiser? More mature?) I once heard guitar virtuoso Eric Clapton explain that when he was younger, in his Cream days, he played many more notes, thinking that was what made a great guitar player. As he got older, he said, he learned it wasn't a matter of playing more notes, "but playing the 'right' ones."

Chili Heat—Measuring Heat

How hot is hot? To the uninitiated, anything that is warmer than a bell pepper is "incendiary." Actually, there is a test that measures the degrees of "hotness" in a chile pepper. It's called the Scoville Organoleptic Test (developed in 1912, naturally enough, by Wilbur Scoville, a pharmaceutical chemist). In the original test, Scoville blended pure ground chiles in a sugar-water solution. A staff of tasters sipped the solution, in increasingly diluted concentrations, until they reached the point where the liquid no longer burned the mouth. Then a number was assigned to each chile based on how much it needed to be diluted before you could not feel the heat.

The heat of chile peppers is measured in multiples of 100 units. One part of chile "heat" per 1 million drops of water rates as only 1.5 Scoville units. The substance that makes a chile so hot is capsaicin. Pure capsaicin rates over 15 million Scoville units!

Note: Keep in mind that the "hotness" of chiles can vary from pod to pod and plant to plant. Even different parts of the same chile pepper can vary to a remarkable degree.

The Chile Thermometer

Scoville units are a common method of measuring the "hotness" of chiles. Sometimes in articles and reports on chile peppers you will also see chiles placed on a chart according to their relative heat measurement, on a scale from 0 to 120, with 0 being the least hot and 120 being the hottest.

The listings on pages 18-19 are an approximation of where many of the chiles called for in this book would fit on such a chart. Where the Scoville Units were available for a particular pepper, I have listed them in parentheses (S.U.). Remember that there is a great deal of variation within a variety, within the peppers on the same plant, and even on the pepper itself. In fact, I remember once biting very cautiously into the tip of a pepper I expected to be quite hot. Surprised at the lack of zip, I took three or four more bites, each surprisingly mild. Suddenly, the next bite nearly blistered

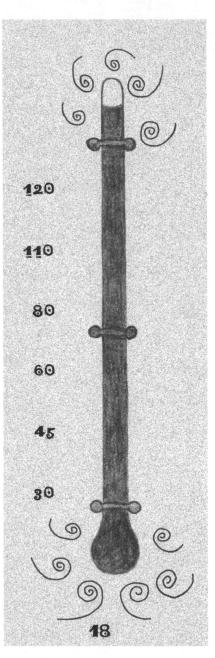

the roof of my mouth! Many chile-philes have similar stories.

120 What chile rates as the hottest, most incendiary, "smoke-comes-out-your-ears" pepper? Well, legend has it there's a little fireball in Thailand that's right up at the top. However, as it's not yet commercially available, most charts I've seen place the habañero (see below) as the hottest commercially available chile, even though it ranks only at 110! I guess they're saving the "120" rating for when the Thai peppers hit the market.

110 HABAÑEROS AND SCOTCH BONNETS ≈ (100,00- 350,000 S.U.) Though some chile experts classify habañeros and Scotch bonnets as two separate varieties, many also consider them the same pepper botanically. This is the hot one!!!!! Although habañeros are blisteringly hot, their effects are short-lived, and according to many chile-heads, quite pleasurable. I enjoy using a very small amount, just a pinch of dried ground habañero or a tiny piece of fresh chile very finely minced, combined with other varieties of chiles in a large pot of soup, stew, chiles, or beans. Or sometimes I'll make a very hot salsa or chutney and serve it on the side for the more adventurous (with warning labels—have some compassion for your guests).

80 SANTAKA, CHILTEPIN, COMMON THAI PEPPER ≈ (50,000-100,000 S.U.) The general rule of thumb is that the smaller the pepper, the more likely it is to be hot. Chiltepins are proof of this rule. Small, BB-sized fruit, these really pack a wallop. One or two chiltepins crushed into a stew will season it very nicely.

60 Aji, Cayenne, Tabasco, Piquin, Tabasco Sauce ≈ (30,000-50,000 S.U.)

45 Chile de Arbol, Santa Fe Grande ≈ (15,000-30,000 S.U.)

30 Yellow Wax, Serrano ≈ (5,000-15,000 S.U.)

20 Mirasol, Guajillo, Crushed Red Pepper Flakes ≈ (3,000-5,000 S.U.) (Guajillo is the dried form of a mirasol pepper.)

15 Jalapeño, Chipotle, Casteno Amarillo, Hatch ≈ (2,500-3,500 S.U.) (A chipotle is a jalapeño that has been smoked and dried.)

10 Sandia, Cascabel, Cherry Peppers; Pepperoncini ≈ (500-2,500 S.U.)

5 Poblano, Ancho, Pasilla, Espanola, Chihuacle negro ≈ (1,000-1,500 S.U.) (An ancho is a dried poblano pepper. Poblanos are the peppers that are stuffed and fried for a dish known as chile relleños.)

3 Anaheim, Big Jim, Canned "Mild" Green Chiles ≈ (500-1,000 S.U.)

1 Mexi-Bells, Cherry, Most Blended Chili Powders ≈ (100-500 S.U.)

0 Red or Green Bell Peppers, Sweet Banana, Pimientos, Paprika ≈ (0-100 S.U.)

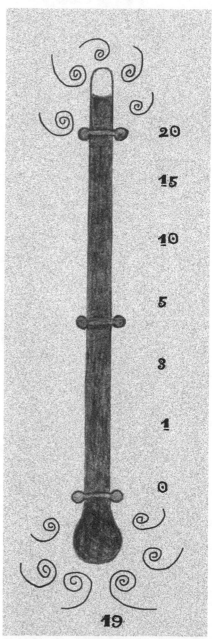

20
15
10
5
3
1
0

19

CHILIS!

The flavor and heat of a chile also are determined by whether it is fresh or dried, green or ripe, and powdered or blended with other spices. Generally, though, the smaller and thinner the pepper, the hotter it will be. Experiment and find the flavors you like best.

(Note: Remember to wear rubber gloves whenever you work with the hotter chiles—and don't rub your eyes or nose!)

How to Use Chiles— Growing Chiles

I've had much success growing chile peppers of many varieties in such vastly different climates as Illinois and Arizona, and I've spoken with enthusiastic chile gardeners throughout most of the United States. In fertile, well-composted soil, plant seeds or small plants outdoors after all danger of frost has passed. Grow alongside tomatoes as a good companion plant. If you don't have space for a garden in your yard, chiles grow very well as a container plant on your patio or deck. I grew some beautiful haba-ñeros, chiltepins, and pasillas in clay pots right outside my back door.

I have found that in Tucson (and probably other areas where frost is only a minor problem) I can grow chiles in a well-protected area of my garden, covering the plants during frost warnings, and I will continue to get fruit most of the year. In fact, though pepper plants are usually considered an annual plant, I've had some plants last three or four years, becoming nice-sized shrubs, before I forgot to cover them some cold, icy night. Even when slightly frozen, though, I've had some plants come back to life after pruning the damaged parts.

Though that shows me how hardy these tough little plants can be, if you live in an area where frost is a real danger and if your plant is not too large, you might even transplant it into a large pot and bring it inside during the colder months. Though they lose a few leaves, they can sometimes survive until you can put them back into the soil in the spring. Of course, this is Arizona I'm talking about, where days are sunny right through winter. If you live anyplace north of, say, Texas, I'd just plan on

21

growing new plants every summer. Just save a few dried seeds from the chiles to plant the next spring.

Remember: Green chiles are an unripened fruit. Because they aren't ripe, they are often more difficult to digest. Red (or yellow, orange, or purple) peppers are the ripened fruit. As peppers ripen, they become sweeter and easier to digest. (Some say hotter, though I haven't noticed a difference.) A pepper won't ripen much after it has been picked, so let it stay on the vine until it reaches the degree of ripeness you desire.

Tips for Drying Chiles

Chiles dry very easily using any of several methods and, once dried, keep for several months when stored in a cool, dry place. If you have access to an electric or solar dehydrator, follow the instructions for that appliance.

To sun-dry chiles (actually a misnomer because they're dried in the shade to prevent color loss), wash and dry chiles and place them on a stainless steel drying tray. I've found that the baking pans used in commercial kitchens work very well, but even a cookie sheet will do. Set a table on an even surface under the shade of a tree or awning. Place the tray on the table with a brick under each corner of the baking sheet so that air will circulate under it. Cover the chiles with muslin or cheesecloth to protect them from insects and birds. Strange as it seems, birds do not taste the heat of the pepper and love them! They will quickly devour a whole tray of chiltepins if they're not protected.

After the peppers have dried outdoors for several days, finish drying them in the oven to destroy any insect eggs and to make sure thicker chiles have dried evenly. Simply place the tray of chiles in a 150°F oven for 30 minutes.

Alternatively, chiles may be easily dried in a gas or electric oven. Set the temperature control at the lowest setting, but not below 150°F. Place cheese-cloth or muslin across the oven racks to keep the chiles from falling through. If using an electric oven, leave the door slightly ajar to let the moisture from the drying peppers escape. If using a gas oven, shut the door; moisture will escape through the flue.

I've found an even easier way, though, that works quite well for me. When the peppers begin to ripen, I place a plastic colander on top of my refrigerator on a heavy plate (to keep my cats from sliding the whole thing onto the floor) and simply place the peppers into the colander as I pick them. Because they're in a colander, loosely placed, the air circulates well around the peppers, and they'll usually dry pretty well in a week or two.

Living in Arizona, we usually depend on swamp coolers and fans to cool our homes in the summer, and this helps with the air circulation as well. If you live in a humid climate, you might have a problem with a black mold that forms. If so, use an oven-drying method. I check them often, rotate them, pull out any that have molded or gone bad and, because they've been put into the colander at different stages, pull out the driest ones and finish them in the oven as described above.

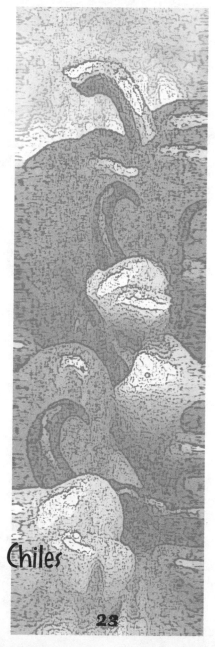

Tips for Buying Chiles

Always look for fresh, firm fruit with no sign of wormholes, mold, or soft spots. Fresh chiles should be fragrant and sweet smelling. (Be very careful when you smell them, though; some people are very sensitive even to the smell of hot chiles.)

Remember that green peppers are not ripe. They do, however, have a longer shelf life and keep a little longer than their ripe vine mates.

Roasting & Peeling Chiles

Fresh chiles should be roasted and peeled before using, as the peels can sometimes be problematic gastronomically for some people. (Canned peppers have already been peeled before canning.) There are several methods for roasting peppers depending on what type of stove or burner you use. Over a gas burner, hold the chile with tongs or on a fork over the full flame. (You might wish to use a pot holder or oven mitt to protect your hand.) Turn the pepper slowly until it becomes black and charred all over. With an electric stove you can toast it under the broiler or in a heavy skillet until, again, the skin chars and blackens. (I have a friend who uses a welder's torch to produce the same results. Not a common kitchen appliance, but it works.)

To remove the skin, place the charred pepper in a bowl of cold water; rub the peel a little and it will come right off. I've had people tell me to place the charred chile in a plastic or paper bag for a few minutes or to put it in the freezer. There are probably as many methods of peeling chiles as there are cooks. Yet I've never found anything easier or more effective than just cooling the pepper in a little water after roasting. The peel comes right off.

Freezing Chiles

Once you've roasted and peeled the chiles, it's a simple matter to place them in plastic freezer bags and place them in the freezer. Frozen peppers will usually last three to six months before they start to suffer from freezer burn. When you need some fresh chiles for a recipe, simply open the bag of frozen chiles, break off the amount you need, and place the rest back into the freezer. Simple!

Removing the Seeds

Some cooks believe that the seeds are hotter than other parts of the pepper. Actually the white membrane, or placenta, to which the seeds are attached, is the hottest part of the pepper. (Though, as I've said, it will differ from pepper to pepper, this is generally the case.) If you feel better removing the seeds, be my guest, though I can't see making the pepper milder than it's supposed to be anyway. Why not just use a milder variety of pepper?

Cooking with Chiles

If you are not sure what your dinner guests' heat tolerance might be or if you know that it is relatively low, play it safe and make your dish milder than you generally would. Remember that it's easier for the fire-lover to add a little cayenne or Tabasco than for the chile-phobe to cool off a too-hot dish.

"Enlightenment embodies compassion. If you're using hot peppers in your dishes, please be merciful and at least inform your guests."

—Baba Bob

25

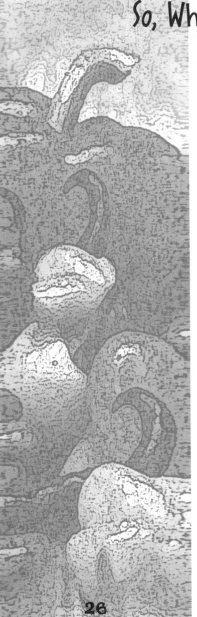

So, What About Chili?

Chili, as opposed to chile, is the term generally applied to a thick stew using fresh or dried chiles as a main ingredient. Traditionally, chili consisted of chunks of meat, usually pork or beef, cooked with onion, garlic, dried ground or fresh chopped chile peppers, and other spices and herbs. This was known as chile con carne, or chile with meat. Eventually the spelling became more Americanized, and some cooks began to add beans (called frijoles in Spanish) to make chile con frijoles. As we move into the millennium, many have decided for health, environmental, economic, or spiritual reasons to forego cooking or eating animals.

Though traditionally chili may have begun as a meat dish, its culinary horizons have expanded. The art of making chili has taken a quantum leap into the future with the use of meat substitutes such as textured soy protein, tofu, seitan, tempeh, or the like; the addition of other vegetables, such as mushrooms, zucchini, and corn; the use of grains such as rice, barley, and amaranth; and even changing the focus of the dish to add ethnic foods from other cultures.

I hope you find the recipes in this book simple and tasty. Experiment, adapt, and modify them to suit you and your family's tastes and needs.

Most of all, enjoy them!

Chile Tips

Water, soda, or even beer are not very effective in putting out the fire of hot chile peppers. They tend to spread the flames rather than put them out. Milk, ice cream, sour cream, or yogurt are probably much better at quenching the pain. Dairy products contain casein which helps to protect the taste buds from the capsaicin found in the chiles. For those with dairy allergies, some soy cheeses contain casein without triggering the symptoms of dairy intolerance. For vegans, you might try soy yogurt, rice beverages, or the like, but I haven't found them to be as effective as dairy yogurt, I'm afraid.

Chile peppers are a wonderful diet food, not simply because they are so low in calories (though that's part of it), but because they add so much flavor to foods that many people find they don't miss the fat and calories. Some studies have shown that chiles increase the body's metabolism and ability to burn fat, though this isn't generally agreed upon.

Chile Powder

Chile powder is usually the dried and ground chile pepper only. Blended chili powder is the dried and ground chile blended with other spices and seasonings such as onion powder, garlic powder, cumin, oregano, and sometimes salt. The recipes in this book generally call for blended chili powder unless otherwise specified.

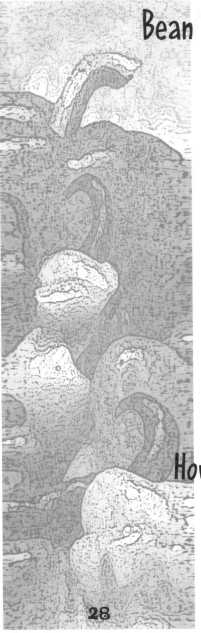

Bean Basics & More

There are, of course, chili purists who wouldn't dream of "contaminating" their chili with the addition of beans. There are also those who don't consider it chili unless it contains animal flesh. Most of the rest of us find the addition of beans to our chili (and the absence of meat) to be just fine. Beans add a wonderful flavor and texture combined with vegetables and, certainly, lots of tasty chiles.

Beans are not only delicious and versatile, they are also a wonderful source of vitamins A, B, and C, calcium, phosphorus, potassium, and iron. One cup of cooked beans contains 13 to 17 grams of protein and less than 1 gram of fat (except soybeans, which have 15 grams of fat per 1 cup serving). Beans are also a good source of fiber, which, combined with their protein content, makes them an excellent alternative to meat (which, by the way, has no fiber).

When buying beans, remember that 1 pound of dry beans measures about 2 cups and yields 6 cups of cooked beans. Dried beans will keep up to a year if stored in an airtight container at room temperature.

How to Cook Beans

Dry beans are notorious for containing small pebbles, field corn, etc. First, pick through the beans well, and discard any foreign object or cracked or misshapen beans.

There are two reasons for soaking beans: it cuts down on the cooking time and removes some of the enzymes that cause flatulence (gas). Cover beans well with fresh, cold water, and soak

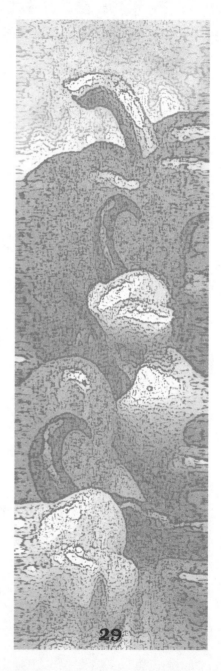

overnight or for several hours. (If you're really in a hurry, you can soak your beans for only a couple of hours—or not at all—but it's much better to soak them at least 8 hours.) After soaking, pour the water off (do not save it) and cover again with fresh, cold water. Bring to a full rolling boil, then reduce to a low boil and cook, partially covered (to let the steam escape so the pot doesn't boil over) for 1 hour or longer, or until the beans are very tender. Caution: Do not add salt or any ingredients containing salt to the beans until they are completely tender. Salt enters the outer layer of the bean and seals it, keeping out the water and steam needed to cook it through.

Preparing beans isn't as time consuming as it may seem. It takes only a little work; the rest of the time the beans are cooking. But if this is still too much for you, try a pressure cooker. A pressure cooker will cut the cooking time by quite a bit.

Almost any bean variety except split peas can be cooked in a pressure cooker. (Split peas tend to foam and clog up the pressure cooker valve.) Beans do not have to be soaked before cooking, but soaking will lessen the cooking time.

To pressure cook beans, add unsoaked dry beans to the cooker with enough fresh water to cover them by about 2 inches. Bring the beans to a boil for 1 minute, and skim off the foam or skins that rise to the top before locking the lid. A good rule is to cook 1 cup beans with 4 cups water and 1 table-spoon oil (which controls foaming). For a 4-quart cooker, you can generally cook 4 cups dried beans; for a 6-quart cooker, you can cook 6 cups. (If cooking soybeans, decrease this quantity to 3 cups and 5 cups, respectively.) Lock on the lid, put on the jig-gle-top or weight, and bring to pressure. Pressure cook beans (at 15 pounds, if your cooker has a

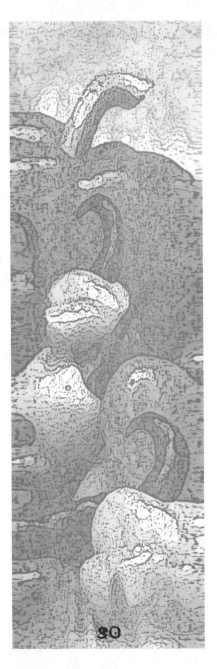

gauge) for about 30 minutes. Different types of beans require slightly different cooking times (soybeans take at least an hour), but on average, most beans will be tender after 25 minutes.

To lessen cooking time, soak the beans in enough water to cover for about 6 to 8 hours, or overnight in the refrigerator. Drain off the soaking water before placing them in the pressure cooker. Follow the instructions for unsoaked beans, but reduce the cooking time by about 5 to 10 minutes. Again, different varieties might require slightly longer or shorter cooking times.

If you have a crock pot, it becomes very simple to put your beans into the crock pot the night before and cover with water. The next morning, pour off the soaking water, cover with fresh water, and turn the crock pot to low. When you come home in the afternoon or evening, the beans will be cooked and ready to use in your favorite recipe.

However you prepare them, make a large pot of beans at a time, put some of the cooked beans in plastic containers or freezer bags, and freeze them. Beans freeze very well and it's simple to thaw them for a quick meal.

A step-saving suggestion: If you're making the beans specifically for a chili recipe, why not just leave your beans in the crock pot, add the rest of the ingredients, and continue to cook your chili right in the crock pot!

Bean Varieties

A small, oval, burgundy-colored bean with a white stripe. Native to the Orient. Easy to digest. Delicate, sweet flavor and soft texture. Use in soups, salads, stir-fries, bean cakes, and pasta dishes. Combines well with winter squash, sweet red pepper, and brown rice. Season with tamari, ginger, or Chinese Five-Spice Seasoning.

Cooking time: 1 hour. Pressure cook soaked beans 15 minutes; unsoaked beans, 20 minutes.

Red and white speckled bean originally cultivated by Native Americans. Loses mottled appearance during cooking. Size and shape similar to pinto bean. Sweet, full flavor and mealy texture. Excellent in Mexican dishes. Use for refried beans, burritos, and bean dips. Combines well with tomatoes, corn, squash, and peppers. Season with garlic, chiles, cilantro, cumin, or coriander.

Cooking time: 1 hour. Pressure cook soaked beans 20 minutes; unsoaked beans, 25 minutes.

Small, round, purple-black bean. A staple of Latin America and the Orient. Distinct, earthy flavor and mealy texture. Excellent in Mexican, Caribbean, and Southwestern dishes. Use in sauces, soups, bean cakes, refried beans, salads, and bean dips. Combines well with tomatoes, corn, avocado, rice, and other grains. Season with garlic, lime juice, chiles, cardamom, cumin, or fresh cilantro.

Cooking time: 1½ hours. Pressure cook soaked beans 20 minutes; unsoaked beans, 30 minutes.

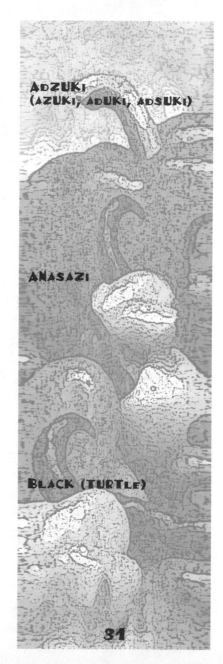

ADZUKI
(AZUKI, ADUKI, ADSUKI)

ANASAZI

BLACK (TURTLE)

31

CRANBERRY

Pink and beige mottled bean related to the kidney bean. Colors fade during cooking. Earthy flavor and mealy texture. Use in soups, stews, bean cakes, refried beans, and casseroles. Combines well with chiles, corn, and squash. Season with garlic or rosemary.

Cooking time: 1 to 1½ hours. Pressure cook soaked beans 20 minutes; unsoaked beans, 25 minutes.

FAVA (BROAD)

Large, flat, kidney-shaped bean. Brown in color. Strong, almost bitter flavor and granular texture. Popular in the Middle East and Italy. Use in soups, stews, and casseroles. Combines well with tomatoes, sweet bell pepper, and dairy or soy parmesan cheese. Season with garlic, chiles, and cumin.

Cooking time: 1 to 1½ hours. Pressure cook soaked beans 20 minutes; unsoaked beans, 25 minutes.

GARBANZO BEANS (CHICK-PEAS)

Medium-sized, round, tan bean with a nutlike flavor and firm texture. Popular in Middle Eastern, Indian, and Mediterranean cooking. Often used in dips (such as hummus), soups, salads, croquettes (falafel), curries, and pasta dishes. Combines well with couscous, winter squash, yams, and eggplant. Season with olive oil, garlic, lemon juice, parsley, rosemary, mint, or cardamom.

Cooking time: 1½ to 2 hours. Pressure cook soaked beans 20 minutes; unsoaked beans, 30 minutes.

LENTIL

Small, disk-shaped seed-like bean. May be yellow, red, green, or brown. Delicate, earthy flavor and creamy texture. Use in soups, salads, purées, dips, pâtés, burgers, and curries. Combines well with most vegetables and grains. Season with garlic, onion, thyme, curry, oregano, and parsley.

Cooking time: 30 to 40 minutes. Pressure cook 10 to 12 minutes. Soaking not required.

Small, oblong, dark olive bean native to India. Delicate, sweet flavor and soft texture. Easy to digest. Use in Indian dals and curries and in Asian soups. Sprouted mung beans are popular in Oriental and Asian cooking. Combines well with rice and Oriental vegetables. Season with curry, tamari, or ginger.

Cooking time: 45 minutes. Pressure cook 20 minutes. Soaking not required.

Oval, pink and brown speckled bean native to Mexico. Color fades to brown during cooking. Full-bodied, earthy flavor and mealy texture. Great for Tex-Mex dishes. Commonly used in refried beans and chili. Combines well with onions, tomatoes, squash, and corn. Season with garlic, chiles, cumin, and cilantro.

Cooking time: 1½ hours. Pressure cook soaked beans 20 minutes; unsoaked beans, 25 minutes.

Dark, reddish brown, mottled bean similar to a pinto. Earthy flavor and mealy texture. Great for Tex-Mex, Mexican, or Southwestern cuisine. Great for refried beans, chili, stews, soups, and casseroles. Combines well with chiles, onions, tomatoes, squash, and corn. Season with garlic, epazote, cumin, cilantro, and oregano.

Cooking time: 1½ hours. Pressure cook soaked beans 20 minutes; unsoaked beans, 25 minutes.

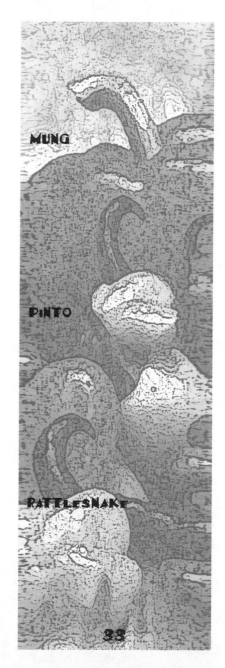

MUNG

PINTO

RATTLESNAKE

33

CHILIS!

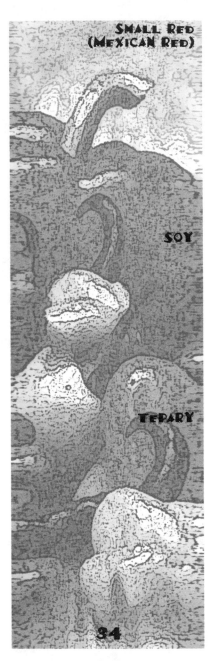

SMALL RED (MEXICAN RED)

SOY

TEPARY

Dark red bean similar to the kidney bean, only smaller. Rich, sweet flavor and mealy texture. Holds shape during cooking. Most often used in soups, salads, chili, refried beans, and Creole dishes. Combines well with tomatoes, corn, and summer squash. Substitute for kidney or pinto beans in any recipe. Season with garlic, onion, chiles, cumin, and cilantro.

Cooking time: 1 to 1½ hours. Pressure cook soaked beans 20 minutes; unsoaked beans, 25 minutes.

Pea-shaped bean native to Central China. May be yellow, green, brown, or black. Mild, nutty flavor and firm texture. Commonly used to make tofu, tempeh, and tamari, soybeans also are great in soups, stew, salads, burgers, and Boston baked beans. Season with garlic, ginger, and tamari.

Cooking time: 3 to 3½ hours. Pressure cook soaked beans 45 minutes; unsoaked beans, 60 minutes.

Small, kidney-shaped beans. Native to Southwest United States. May be white or brown. Earthy, nutty flavor and firm texture. Used for refried beans and chili. Combines well with onion, tomatoes, corn, and squash. Season with garlic, chiles, cumin, and cilantro.

Cooking time: 1½ to 2 hours. Pressure cook soaked beans 25 minutes; unsoaked beans, 30 minutes.

Oblong, cream-colored beans of varying sizes. Mild flavor and slightly granular texture. Interchange-able in most recipes. Use in soups, stews, casseroles, and Boston baked beans. Cannellini are delectable in Italian-style salads and pasta dishes. Combine well with celery, carrots, bell peppers, and tomatoes. Season with garlic, basil, rosemary, thyme, or oregano.

Cooking time: 1½ hours. Pressure cook soaked beans 25 minutes; unsoaked beans, 30 minutes.

Specialty and Heritage Beans

The following are just a few of the specialty and heritage beans available.

Available from Indian Harvest (see page 23):

Appaloosa Beans
Good Mother Stallard Beans
Red Nightfall Beans
Nightfall Beans
Pebble Beans
Tiger Eye Beans
Speckled Brown Cow Beans

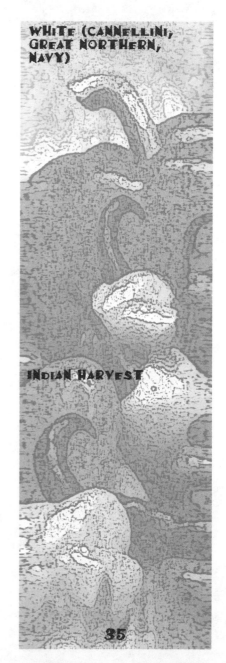

WHITE (CANNELLINI, GREAT NORTHERN, NAVY)

INDIAN HARVEST

35

CHILIS!

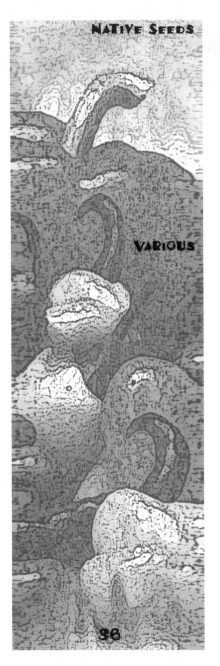

Available from Native Seeds/SEARCH (see page 123):

Anasazi Beans
Colorado River Beans
Dos Mesas Beans
Rio Zape Beans
Brown Tepary Beans
White Tepary Beans
Yellow Eye Beans

Other beans you might find if you look awhile:

Scarlet Runner Beans
Soldier Beans
Flageolet Beans
Black Garbanzo Beans
Black or Green Lentils

Note: Cook these and any unknown variety of beans similar to pintos, and you generally won't go wrong.

Notes on the Ingredients

✔ *Always choose organic foods whenever they are available.*

✔ *Avoid irradiated foods, genetically altered or enhanced foods, artificial sweeteners, artificial fats, etc.*

✔ *Support local farmers, growers, co-ops, non-profits, and small businesses whenever possible.*

Grains, Nuts & Seeds

Amaranth – A wonderful small grain sacred to the Aztecs. Quite nutritious and flavorful, it grows well in some home gardens, especially in the Southwest. It is readily available in most any health food store or co-op.

Barley – Nutty, sweet flavored, and chewy, barley is a popular grain found in any health food store or co-op. Also available in groceries, where it is generally not organic.

Bulgur – Quick-cooking cracked wheat commonly used in Middle Eastern and Mediterranean cooking.

Carob – I know I'm in the minority, but I much prefer good carob to chocolate any day. To me, it simply tastes more satisfying, earthy, and rich. Carob powder and prepared carob candies are available in most health food stores and co-ops. Some

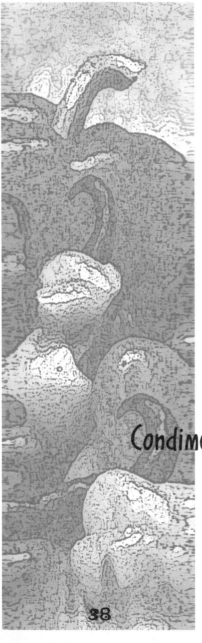

brands, Carafection and Sunspire among them, taste better to me than others.

Cashews – These and other nuts should be organic, of course, and preferably raw and unsalted.

Chocolate – If you do use chocolate, be sure it is organic and natural, at least, with a minimum of flavorings and food additives. There are now some high-quality cocoa and chocolate products available in health food stores and co-ops.

Peanut butter – Buy only real peanut butter with no ingredients other than peanuts. Especially avoid brands with hydrogenated fats.

Quinoa – Similar in size to amaranth but with a very different flavor. You might substitute quinoa for amaranth.

Rice – I prefer long- or short-grain brown rice or brown basmati rice for most recipes, but sometimes for special flavor and aroma, you might try white basmati or jasmine rice.

Condiments & Packaged Ingredients

Artichoke hearts – Usually found in small jars in the condiment section of supermarkets, artichoke hearts usually come marinated in either water or oil with herbs and seasonings. If you're watching your fat intake, choose the water-packed.

Balsamic vinegar – Made from high-quality grapes and aged in wooden vats for several years, balsamic vinegar is much more flavorful than most other vinegars. Available in supermarkets and health food stores.

Barbecue sauce – There are many tasty sauces on the market now, but watch to see if Worcestershire sauce is listed as an ingredient because it often contains anchovies. Gorilla Sauce is one brand I've used and liked.

Brown rice vinegar – A tasty, mild vinegar made from brown rice. Found primarily in health food stores.

Canned tomato products – Muir Glen or Millina's make a fine line of organic canned tomatoes.

Nutritional yeast – A food supplement flake or powder that lends a cheesy, nutty flavor, as well as lots of B vitamins, to any dish. Because it is a non-active yeast, it is acceptable for use by people on yeast-free diets.

Seitan – Available in several styles and varieties in health food stores and Oriental markets. It is sold already prepared in jars and packages and comes in several flavors. There is also a seitan mix put out by Arrowhead Mills that makes wonderful seitan very inexpensively. If using this mix, add a teaspoon of blended chili powder to the dry ingredients to give it an even more authentic flavor.

Sun-dried tomatoes – These are usually packaged dry, either in halves or pieces, and are usually found in the produce section. They need to be rehydrated before using, unless you're cooking them in a dish like soup or chili. The recipes in this

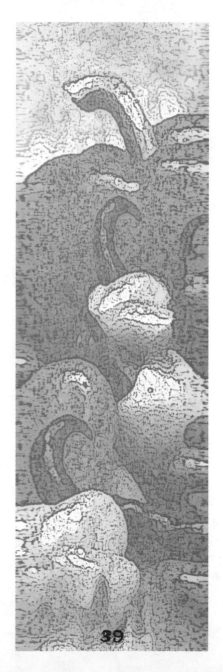

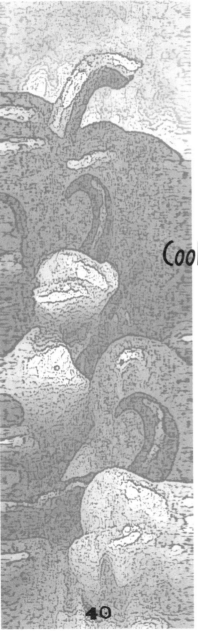

book call for the dried tomatoes. Sometimes you will see them jarred in olive oil, but the extra fat is not needed.

Tamari or soy sauce – In Japan, tamari is a wheat-free soy sauce and shoyu is a soy sauce containing wheat. In the United States, they're both just generally called soy sauce. If you're on a wheat-free diet, read the label. I find tamari to have a richer flavor than shoyu. Avoid cheap "imitation" soy sauces, generally the ones found in supermarkets. Eden and San-J make high-quality organic soy sauces that are found in health food stores, co-ops, and in some larger supermarkets.

Cooking Oils & Tips

✔ *Always look for cold- or expeller-pressed oils, preferably in glass bottles. Store all oils in a cool, dry, dark place (the refrigerator if there is room), and toss them out at the first sign of rancidity. Spectrum and Hain are suggested brands; for sesame oil, try Eden.*

Canola oil – Made from a plant called rapeseed, most of which is grown in Canada (hence Canadian oil, or Canola). This mild oil works well as an all-purpose cooking oil.

Hot sesame oil – Just like toasted sesame oil with the addition of oils from hot peppers.

Olive oil – Always buy extra-virgin if it is available. Avoid "lite" olive oil; it is merely light in color and has less flavor. Look for a dark green oil packed in a dark glass bottle.

Toasted sesame oil – Has an unique nutty flavor that really enhances dishes when used in small amounts.

Spices, Herbs & Seasonings

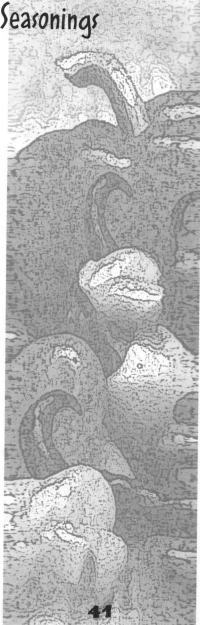

Basil – Though not often used in Mexican or Southwestern cooking, basil does compliment tomato dishes well and is included in a few recipes in this book. Unless fresh basil is specified in the recipe, dried basil is called for. You may substitute fresh basil for the dried, if you prefer, but keep in mind that dried herbs are generally stronger or more concentrated in flavor, usually about three times as strong as fresh. One teaspoon dried basil is equivalent to 1 tablespoon fresh.

Bay leaves – Leave them whole so they may be picked out before eating.

Cilantro – Cilantro is to chili what basil is to pasta sauce. Cilantro is actually the leaf of the coriander plant and has a distinct flavor that some people simply do not care for. Therefore, in many of the recipes in this book, I use cilantro more as a garnish than as an ingredient. That way you can leave it out if someone doesn't like it.

Dried cilantro is usually quite tasteless and is best avoided; always buy fresh. Fresh herbs tend to lose their flavor quite rapidly in cooking and are best added at the end of the cooking process, but please do not substitute coriander for cilantro. Coriander usually refers to the ground seed of the plant and has a very different flavor.

Cinnamon – Cinnamon is often used in moles or with chocolate in Mexican and Southwestern cuisine and adds a subtle flavor when used in small amounts in some of the recipes in this book.

Coffee – Coffee lends an earthy flavor to chili, the same way chocolate does to a mole sauce. It's also

41

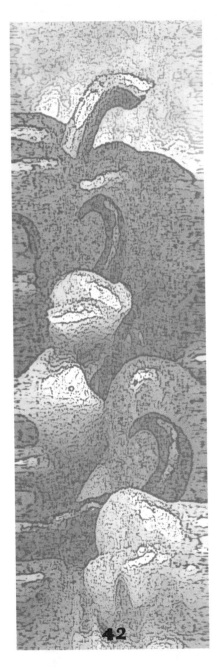

a traditional "cowboy" addition to redeye chili. Of course, organic decaf coffees are more healthful than commercial caffeinated varieties. Many health food stores and co-ops also carry coffees grown by "grower-cooperatives," a political and economic advantage for the small grower in Third World countries.

Cumin – Known as cumino in Spanish, this flavorful herb is essential to chili, almost as much as the chiles themselves. Cumin is not at all hot but does have an interesting, quite intense flavor. The recipes in this book call for ground cumin. If you have the whole seeds, process them in a coffee/spice mill until finely ground.

Curry powder – A blend of many different spices and herbs; use your favorite variety. If you are adept at making your own blend of curry, be my guest. If not, there are a number of good blends available at health food stores, co-ops, gourmet markets, and grocery stores.

Epazote – A traditional herb used in bean dishes by Mexican and Native American cooks, epazote is somewhat new to American cooks and may be difficult to find in some areas of the country. It not only adds an interesting flavor, but it also is reputed to alleviate some of the problems with flatulence for which beans are so famous.

Gomasio – Ground sesame seeds and salt, used as a flavoring.

Grain beverage – Usually chicory-based, with other grains and flavors added, these are blended to simulate the taste of coffee. Again, I confess, I like the taste of grain beverages such as Pero and Cafix better than the taste of coffee.

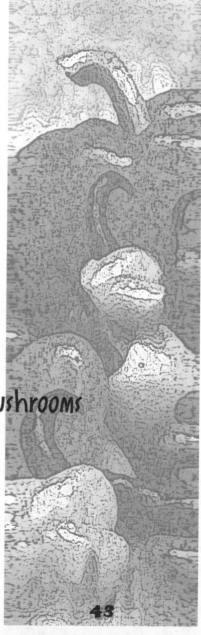

Nutmeg, cloves, and/or allspice – In this book, these spices are usually used along with cinnamon in very small amounts.

Oregano – Unlike basil, oregano is commonly used in Mexican dishes, including chili. Like basil, use dried oregano unless fresh is specified. One teaspoon dried oregano is equivalent to 1 tablespoon fresh.

Salt – Although most studies have shown that there's very little nutritional difference between sea salt and regular table salt, I tend to buy high-quality sea salt for the trace minerals it contains.

Vegetarian "chicken" broth powder – A blend of herbs and seasonings usually associated with poultry dishes (sometimes with the addition of nutritional yeast), this powder is used to thicken and season dishes as a substitute for chicken stock.

Vegetarian "beef" broth powder – Similar to the vegetarian "chicken" broth powder, but with flavors to simulate "beef."

Vegetables / Mushrooms

Button mushrooms – The common white mushrooms found in most supermarkets and produce departments. While not as tasty or well-textured as shiitakes and portabellas, they make a nice addition to many dishes, including chilis.

Portabella mushrooms – Another wonderful mushroom rapidly becoming available in health food stores and produce markets. Portabellas (also called portobellos and spelled in various ways) are

43

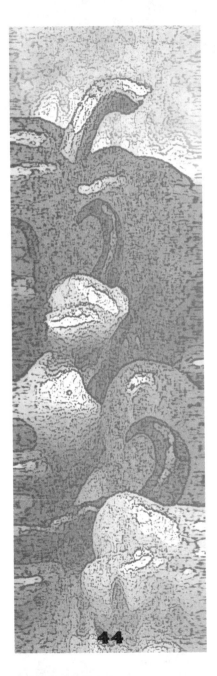

large mushrooms, often several inches across, and boast a wonderful, meaty flavor and texture.

Shiitake mushrooms – Shiitakes are a delicious, thick-textured mushroom. Originally from Japan, shiitakes are now available in many supermarkets, and there are even kits available for growing fresh shiitakes in your home. If you cannot find fresh shiitakes, look in the Asian food section in your market for dried shiitakes. They aren't quite as tasty, but they will do.

Vegetable stock – It's simple and economical to make your own vegetable stock. Simply save any and all non-moldy scraps when preparing vegetables—tomato cores, the butt end of celery or carrots, onion peels, etc.—and place them in a bag or container in your refrigerator or freezer. About once a week or whenever you've accumulated enough scraps, place them in a pot and cover with fresh filtered water. Bring to a boil and then reduce the heat to simmer. Cook about 20 minutes. Save the liquid—that's the stock. Discard the vegetable scraps. Another method is to save the steaming/boiling water from cooking carrots, celery, parsnips, etc. (Avoid too many vegetables from the cabbage family—cabbage, broccoli, kale, cauliflower, etc.—they're too strongly flavored.) Vegetable stock freezes well in freezer bags or containers.

Vegetable juice – Either freshly squeezed (if you have access to a juicer) or bottled (something like V-8), preferably organic.

Water – Use filtered or distilled.

Mexican Ingredients

Masa harina or cornmeal – Terms used interchangeably, masa or cornmeal is sometimes added to soups and stews to thicken them.

Posole – Corn that has been treated with lime. You can sometimes find posole in Mexican markets. If not, substitute hominy instead. They're almost exactly the same.

45

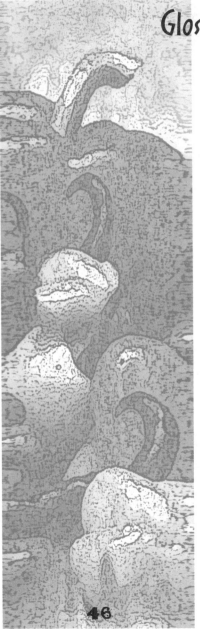

Glossary of Terms

Al dente: Literally "to the tooth." Usually refers to pasta or vegetables and means that the end product is firm and chewy.

Baste: To moisten with a sauce, marinade, or the natural juices of the food being cooked.

Blend: To mix together two or more ingredients well.

Boil: To heat water or other cooking liquid until bubbles come rapidly to the surface and then pop. Also refers to cooking foods in the boiling liquid.

Chop: To cut foods with a chef's or French knife or with a cleaver. Generally the point or front end of the knife is left on the cutting board, and the food is cut with the back part of the knife using a rocking motion with just a slight push forward. Chopped foods are generally a little larger than diced foods, and diced foods are larger than minced.

Dice: To cut into small, square pieces (smaller than chopped).

Garnish: To add a decoration.

Grate: To rub over the surface of a grater. Graters generally have different-sized openings, and each will give a finer or coarser end product depending on the size of the hole.

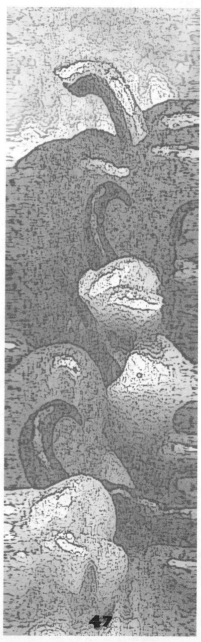

Marinate: To cover a food with a liquid or sauce and let it sit for a time in order to flavor the food.

Mince: To chop very finely (finer than diced).

Preheat: To allow the oven to reach a set temperature before placing food into it.

Sauté: To very quickly fry in a small amount of oil over a fairly high heat. With the increase in health-consciousness these days, some cooks are now "sautéing" by steaming foods in a small amount of liquid.

Simmer: The liquid for cooking is brought to a full boil, and then the temperature is reduced until the liquid barely bubbles.

Steam: To cook food in a covered pan with a steamer basket or other method of keeping the food above the surface of the boiling liquid.

Stew: To simmer for a long time in a covered pot or crock pot.

Whisk: To stir, beat, or whip using a wire whisk.

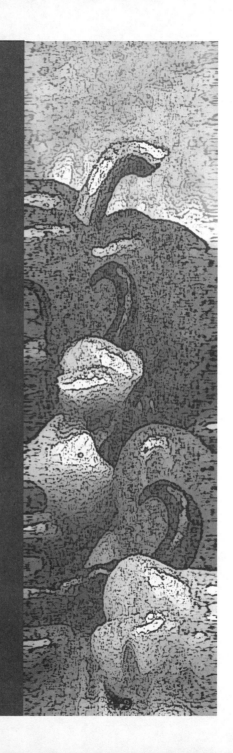

BASIC CHILIS

Basic Vegetarian Chili • 51
Camper's Chili • 52
Chili Mac • 53
Hearty Trucker's Chili • 54
Easy 5-Minute Chili • 55
Five-Bean Chili • 56
Soybean Chili • 58

BASIC VEGETARIAN CHILI

Yield: 4 servings

This is pretty much the basic chili recipe. Experiment. Let your imagination run wild, and add your own favorite ingredients.

Perhaps some mushrooms, squash, or other vegetables? More or other chiles? Unusual ingredients such as olives, peaches (don't knock it 'til you've tried it), or whatever your imagination leads you to.

Combine all of the ingredients, except the cilantro and garnishes, in a large pot or Dutch oven. Cover and bring to a slow boil. Remove the cover and reduce the heat to a low simmer. Cook for 40 minutes.

Add the cilantro just before serving. Garnish with cheese and onion, if desired. Enjoy!

3 cups cooked pinto or kidney beans

1 medium yellow onion, chopped

1 green or red bell pepper, diced

2 tomatoes, chopped

1 cup tomato sauce

1 tablespoon chili powder

½ teaspoon ground cumin

2 cloves garlic, minced

1 Anaheim chile, roasted, peeled, and minced

¼ cup minced fresh cilantro

Grated dairy or soy cheese and chopped red onion, for garnish

Per serving: Calories 224, Protein 10 g, Fat 0 g, Carbohydrates 43 g

1 (15-ounce) vegetarian chili beans

1 (15-ounce) can chopped or crushed tomatoes

1 medium yellow onion, chopped

2 cloves garlic, minced

1 (15-ounce) can whole kernel corn

2 tablespoons chili powder

Salt and pepper, to taste

1 (12-ounce) bottle Mexican beer (optional)

Water, to cover

CAMPER'S CHILI

Yield: 4 servings

A great backpacker's chili (substitute dehydrated onions and garlic for the real thing) or the basic chili for camping. You just can't beat a good "bowl o' red" while sitting around a blazing campfire.

Combine all the ingredients in a pot, cover, and place it over the campfire or campstove burner. Stir often until heated through. Enjoy!

Per serving: Calories 265, Protein 11 g, Fat 0 g, Carbohydrates 54 g

CHILI MAC

Yield: 4 servings

My mother used to make something like this when we were kids, and we just couldn't get enough of it. Now, of course, I use textured soy protein instead of hamburger; otherwise, it's pretty close to "what Mom used to make." Serve with hot, crusty French bread.

In a large pot or Dutch oven, heat the oil over medium-high heat. Add the onion and cook 3 to 5 minutes, stirring frequently.

Add bell pepper and garlic, and cook 3 minutes.

Add all of the remaining ingredients, except the cilantro, parsley, pasta, and garnishes. Cover and bring to a boil. Reduce the heat to a simmer, and cook, uncovered, for 30 minutes, stirring occasionally.

Stir in the cilantro and parsley just before serving. Serve over the pasta. Garnish with the cheese and scallions, if desired. Enjoy!

*You may substitute 2 cups unflavored tex-tured soy granules + ¼ cup tamari or soy sauce for the beef-style textured soy granules.

Per serving: Calories 623, Protein 38 g, Fat 7 g, Carbohydrates 97 g

2 tablespoons olive oil

1 medium yellow onion, chopped

1 red or green bell pepper, diced

3 cloves garlic, minced

1 (15-ounce) can tomato sauce

1 (6-ounce) can tomato paste

2 cups ground beef-style textured soy granules*

¼ cup minced canned jalapeño chiles

1 tablespoon chili powder

1 teaspoon ground cumin

3 cups cooked pinto beans

Vegetable stock or water, to cover

Salt and pepper, to taste

1 tablespoon minced cilantro

1 tablespoon minced parsley

1 pound spaghetti or macaroni, cooked al dente

Grated Monterey Jack or Asiago cheese and chopped scallions, for garnish

- 2 cups beef-style textured soy granules, or 2 cups unflavored soy granules plus ¼ cup tamari or soy sauce
- 1 large yellow onion, chopped
- 2 cups fresh or frozen corn
- 2 (8-ounce) cans diced or crushed tomatoes
- 1 green and 1 red bell pepper, diced
- 3 cloves garlic, minced
- 1 (6-ounce) can tomato paste
- ¼ cup blended chili powder
- 1 or 2 (4-ounce) cans jalapeño chiles, chopped
- 1 (12-ounce) bottle Mexican beer
- 1 cup papaya juice
- 2 cups cooked pinto beans
- 2 cups cooked red kidney beans
- 1 to 2 dashes Tabasco sauce
- Salt and pepper, to taste
- Dairy or soy cheddar cheese, minced fresh cilantro, and chopped red onions, for garnish

HEARTY TRUCKER'S CHILI

Yield: 4 to 6 servings

This thick, hearty chili will satisfy most any "meat and potatoes" guy. In fact, unless I tell them, most people don't realize the soy granules aren't meat. The papaya juice acts as a tenderizer, as well as adding a subtle, sweet flavor. Serves 6 regular eaters or 4 truckers.

Combine all the ingredients in a large pot or Dutch oven. Cover and bring to a low boil over medium-high heat. Reduce the heat to a simmer, and cook for 40 minutes.

Garnish with cheese, cilantro, and onions, if desired. Enjoy!

Per serving: Calories 460, Protein 30 g, Fat 1 g, Carbohydrates 77 g

Easy Five-Minute Chili

Yield: 4 servings

You can't get much easier than this unless you buy it already made. This is great for a quick meal or for singles not wanting to dirty a lot of utensils. It's also pretty darn good (and gets better when reheated).

Combine all of the ingredients in a large pot or Dutch oven, and bring to a slow boil. Reduce the heat to a simmer, and cook 10 minutes.

Enjoy!

2 (16-ounce) cans cooked vegetarian chili beans

1 (15-ounce) can stewed tomatoes

1 (4-ounce) can chopped mild chiles

1 (16-ounce) can whole kernel corn

1 teaspoon blended chili powder

1 teaspoon garlic powder

1 teaspoon onion powder

1 (12-ounce) bottle Mexican beer (optional)

Salt and pepper, to taste

1 to 2 dashes Tabasco sauce

Per serving: Calories 313, Protein 12 g, Fat 0 g, Carbohydrates 64 g

1 medium onion, chopped

1 red or green bell pepper, diced

1 tablespoon olive oil

2 cloves garlic, minced

1 cup cooked dark red kidney beans

1 cup cooked black beans

1 cup cooked white beans (cannellini, great Northern or navy)

½ cup cooked garbanzo beans

½ cup cooked cranberry beans

1 cup fresh or frozen corn

1 (6-ounce) can tomato paste

1 (15-ounce) can tomato sauce

56

FIVE-BEAN CHILI

Yield: 6 servings

Use any five beans you like; you can't go wrong. (Unless you don't like beans—but then, who doesn't like beans?)

In a large pot or Dutch oven, combine the onion and bell pepper with the oil, and sauté 2 to 3 minutes, stirring often.

Add the garlic and sauté 1 minute more.

1 tablespoon blended chili powder

1 teaspoon ground cumin

1 teaspoon minced fresh basil

2 small dried chiletepins, crushed

1 dried chipotle chile, crushed

Vegetable stock or water, to cover

Salt and pepper, to taste

2 teaspoons minced fresh cilantro

Grated dairy or soy cheddar cheese and chopped scallions, for garnish

Add all of the remaining ingredients, except the cilantro and garnishes, and bring to a boil. Reduce the heat to a low simmer, and cook for 40 minutes, stirring occasionally.

Add the cilantro just before serving. Garnish with cheese and scallions, if desired. Enjoy!

Per serving: Calories 261, Protein 22 g, Fat 4 g, Carbohydrates 46 g

Ingredients

2 tablespoons olive oil

1 medium yellow onion, chopped

3 tomatoes, chopped

3 cloves garlic, minced

2 fresh Anaheim chiles, roasted, peeled, and minced

2 cups cooked soybeans

1 (16-ounce) can tomato purée

1 (15-ounce) can hominy

1 tablespoon blended chili powder

Pinch cayenne

Vegetable stock or water, to cover

Salt and pepper, to taste

⅓ cup minced fresh cilantro

Grated soy or dairy pepper Jack cheese and diced onions, for garnish

SOYBEAN CHILI

Yield: 4 servings

Soybeans are a wonderful source of nutrition, a true power food. They're also quite tasty, as this chili shows. Leftovers are also quite good wrapped in a whole wheat tortilla for a quick soy burrito!

Heat the oil over medium-high heat in a large pot or Dutch oven. Add the onion and sauté until the onion is translucent, about 5 minutes. Add the tomatoes, garlic, and chiles, and sauté another 3 minutes. Stir often to prevent sticking.

Add all of the remaining ingredients, except the cilantro and garnishes; cover and bring to a slow boil. Remove the cover, reduce the heat to a simmer, and cook 30 minutes.

Stir in the cilantro before serving. Garnish with cheese and onions, if desired. Enjoy!

Per serving: Calories 389, Protein 17 g, Fat 13 g, Carbohydrates 48 g

TRADITIONAL CHILIS

Coyote Chili • 61
Four Corners Chili • 62
Potato Chili • 63
Calabacitas Chili • 64
Greenhouse Chili • 65
Posole Chili • 66
Cactus Chili • 67
Pacifico Chili • 68
Tex-Mex Chili Mac • 69
Juan's Chili • 70
Green Chili Stew • 71
Chili Mole • 72
Texas White Chili • 73
Sedona Redeye Chili • 74
Black Bean & Butternut Squash Chili • 75

COYOTE CHILI

Yield: 4 servings

While perhaps not quite an authentic Native American recipe, this tasty chili follows the spirit of the wonderful ingredients of the Southwest. Serve this for a special fiesta or celebration, but guard it carefully or the cunning coyote might come and steal it! Serve with coleslaw, corn on the cob, and lots of chips and salsa!

1 red onion, chopped

4 tomatoes, chopped

1 yellow summer squash, diced

1 cup cooked red corn posole

2 cloves garlic, minced

1 Anaheim chile, roasted, peeled, and minced

¼ cup minced fresh cilantro

2 teaspoons chipotle chili powder

1 teaspoon ground cumin

1 teaspoon epazote (optional)

2 cups cooked Rio Zape or black beans

½ cup raw sunflower seeds

¼ cup masa harina or cornmeal

Vegetable stock, to cover

Salt and pepper, to taste

Grated dairy or soy cheddar cheese and blue corn chips, for garnish

Combine all of the ingredients, except the garnishes, in a large pot or Dutch oven, and bring to a boil. Reduce the heat to a simmer, cover, and cook 40 minutes, stirring frequently. If the chili becomes too dry or too thick, add a little water, stock, or vegetable juice.

Garnish with cheese and chips, if desired. Enjoy!

Per serving: Calories 311, Protein 13 g, Fat 10 g, Carbohydrates 43 g

2 cups beef-style textured soy chunks, or 2 cups unflavored soy chunks + ¼ cup tamari or soy sauce

2 cups cooked red corn posole

1 medium yellow onion, chopped

4 tomatoes, chopped

1 large or 2 small yellow summer squash, chopped

2 cloves garlic, minced

2 dried pasilla chiles, crushed

1 tablespoon blended chili powder

¼ cup masa harina or cornmeal

2 cups cooked dos mesas or pinto beans

Vegetable stock or water, to cover

Salt and pepper, to taste

Minced fresh cilantro and crumbled goat cheese or feta cheese, for garnish

FOUR CORNERS CHILI

Yield: 4 servings

This dish is based on Native American chilis and stews from the Four Corners region of the United States, where the states of Arizona, New Mexico, Utah, and Colorado meet. The soy chunks take the place of the mutton usually found in Navajo and Hopi dishes. Have a stack of hot wheat or corn tortillas handy with this flavorful chili.

Combine all of the ingredients, except the garnishes, in a large pot or Dutch oven, and bring to a low boil. Reduce the heat to a simmer, and cook 1 hour, stirring occasionally. Add stock or water if it gets too thick.

Garnish with cilantro and cheese, if desired. Enjoy!

Per serving: Calories 402, Protein 30 g, Fat 1 g, Carbohydrates 67 g

POTATO CHILI

Yield: 4 servings

This versatile chili is good with or without beans. (You might add some pintos or anasazi beans if you like.) Believe it or not, this also goes quite well with scrambled tofu for breakfast. Leftovers are quite good wrapped in a whole wheat tortilla for an interesting burrito.

4 large unpeeled russet potatoes, chopped

1 medium onion, chopped

1 red bell pepper, chopped

2 small carrots, chopped

1 stalk celery, chopped

4 tomatoes, chopped

1 cup fresh or frozen corn

1 (4-ounce) can mild chiles

1 tablespoon blended chili powder

Pinch dried dill (optional)

Tomato juice, to cover

Salt and pepper, to taste

Sour cream, grated dairy or soy cheese, and minced fresh cilantro, for garnish

Combine all of the ingredients, except the garnishes, in a large pot or Dutch oven, cover, and bring to a low boil. Reduce the heat to a simmer, and cook until the chili is fairly thick, about 40 minutes.

Garnish with sour cream, cheese, and cilantro, if desired. Enjoy!

Variation: Delete the potatoes from the recipe, and serve the chili over a baked potato for a hearty and filling meal.

Per serving: Calories 278, Protein 5 g, Fat 0 g, Carbohydrates 63 g

1 large or 2 small zucchini, diced

2 small yellow summer squash, diced

4 tomatoes, chopped

1 medium yellow onion, chopped

1 green and 1 red bell pepper, diced

1 cup fresh or frozen corn

2 fresh hatch chiles, roasted, peeled, and diced

1 teaspoon blended chili powder

Juice of 2 limes

½ cup cooked black beans

⅓ cup minced fresh cilantro

Grated dairy or soy cheddar cheese, chopped scallions, and black olives, for garnish

CALABACITAS CHILI

Yield: 4 servings

Calabacitas means "squash" in Spanish, and this delicious squash chili is one of my favorites. Serve as is, or, for a really tasty burrito, roll some of the chili with grated cheese in a whole wheat tortilla. Cornbread is a tasty addition too.

Combine all of the ingredients, except the cilantro and garnishes, in a large pot or Dutch oven. Cover and bring to a low boil. Reduce the heat to a simmer, and cook, uncovered, for 30 minutes, stirring often.

Add the cilantro just before serving. Garnish with cheese, scallions, and olives, if desired. Enjoy!

Per serving: Calories 135, Protein 5 g, Fat 0 g, Carbohydrates 27 g

Greenhouse Chili

Yield: 25 servings

This is the chili for which the Greenhouse Café in Cottonwood, Arizona, is justly known. This recipe makes a pretty large amount, but it freezes very well. Better yet, make it for a large party, complete with cornbread.

In a very large pot, combine the onions and bell peppers in the oil over medium heat. Cover and cook, stirring often, until the vegetables are tender, about 10 minutes.

Add all of the remaining ingredients, except the garnishes, and cook slowly, uncovered, over low heat for 25 to 30 minutes. Garnish with cilantro and sour cream, if desired. Enjoy!

* Bragg Liquid Aminos is a soy flavoring that looks and tastes like soy sauce but is a little lower in sodium and is not fermented.

Per serving: Calories 262, Protein 17 g, Fat 5 g, Carbohydrates 37 g

6 cups chopped yellow onions

4 cups chopped green bell peppers

2 cups chopped red bell peppers

½ cup canola oil

10 cloves garlic, minced

¼ cup ground cumin

½ cup hatch chili powder

2 tablespoons dried oregano

6 tablespoons vegetarian "beef" broth powder

6 cups beef-style textured soy chunks, or 6 cups unflavored textured soy chunks + ¾ cup tamari or soy sauce

6 cups frozen corn

2 tablespoons salt

4 teaspoons black pepper

3 cups canned chopped tomatoes

3 cups tomato sauce

½ cup Bragg Liquid Aminos*

16 cups water

10 cups cooked pinto beans

Minced fresh cilantro and sour cream, for garnish

65

2 cups cooked posole

1 cup textured beef-style soy chunks, or 1 cup unflavored textured soy chunks + 2 tablespoons tamari or soy sauce

½ teaspoon liquid smoke (optional)

1 large yellow onion, chopped

4 tomatoes, chopped

1 (15-ounce) can tomato sauce

2 yellow summer squash, diced

2 cloves garlic, minced

1 dried costeno Amarillo chile, crushed

1 (12-ounce) bottle Mexican beer (optional)

Vegetable stock, to cover

Salt and pepper, to taste

Grated pepper-Jack cheese and minced fresh cilantro, for garnish

POSOLE CHILI

Yield: 4 servings

Posole is to the Mexican and Native American cultures what hominy is to the South. In fact, if you can't find posole in your neck of the woods, either order some from the Sources section (pages 122-124) or substitute canned vegetarian hominy in its place. There are no beans in this recipe, but if you like, add a cup or two of cooked pintos or kidney beans. Serve with plenty of hot corn tortillas.

Combine all of the ingredients, except the garnishes, in a large pot or Dutch oven. Cover and bring to a boil. Remove the cover, reduce the heat to a simmer, and cook for 40 minutes.

Garnish with cheese and cilantro, if desired. Enjoy!

Per serving: Calories 218, Protein 14 g, Fat 0 g, Carbohydrates 38 g

CACTUS CHILI

Yield: 4 servings

Of course visitors to the Southwest always marvel at the beauty and abundance of cacti in the desert, but not many realize that the paddles of the prickly pear or nopal cactus may be peeled and cooked to make a tasty side dish or addition to a recipe. No need to brave the sharp needles, though, as canned varieties (called nopalitos or nopales) are available in the Mexican food section of many markets, sans needles. They usually come already seasoned or in a thin tomato sauce; just add the entire can to the recipe.

2 (6-ounce) cans chopped nopalitos (cooked cactus paddles)

2 cups cooked brown tepary beans

1 cup chicken-style textured soy chunks, or 1 cup unflavored textured soy chunks + 1 teaspoon vegetarian "chicken" broth powder

4 tomatoes, chopped,

1 medium yellow onion, chopped

1 (12-ounce) bottle Mexican beer (optional)

1 dried ancho chile, crushed

1 cup cooked blue corn posole or hominy

2 cloves garlic, minced

1 dried pasilla chile, crushed

1 tablespoon blended chili powder

½ teaspoon epazote (optional)

Vegetable stock, to cover

2 tablespoons minced fresh cilantro

Sour cream and lime wedges, for garnish

Combine all of the ingredients, except the cilantro and garnishes, in a large pot or Dutch oven; cover and bring to a low boil. Uncover, reduce the heat to a simmer, and cook for 40 minutes.

Add the cilantro just before serving. Garnish with sour cream and lime wedges, if desired. Enjoy!

Per serving: Calories 327, Protein 19 g, Fat 0 g, Carbohydrates 60 g

1 cup beef-style textured soy chunks, or 1 cup unflavored textured soy chunks + 2 tablespoons tamari or soy sauce

1 medium yellow onion, chopped

2 to 3 cloves garlic, minced

4 tomatoes, chopped

1 cup fresh or frozen corn

1 (15-ounce) can Mexican-style stewed tomatoes

1 (12-ounce) bottle Mexican beer

3 cups cooked anasazi beans

¼ cup canned minced jalapeño chiles

¼ cup minced fresh cilantro

Juice of 2 limes

Sour cream, chopped scallions, and grated pepper Jack cheese, for garnish

PACIFICO CHILI

Yield: 4 servings

Bottled beer, especially a good Mexican variety, makes not only a good accompaniment to chili, it is often an essential ingredient to the stew itself. Much of the alcohol cooks away, but it leaves behind a wonderful flavor that compliments the hot peppers and seasonings well. Serve this chili with corn tortillas, especially the thick ones called "gorditos," and, of course, another beer.

Combine all of the ingredients, except the cilantro, lime juice, and garnishes, in a large pot or Dutch oven, and bring to a low boil. Reduce the heat and simmer for 40 minutes, stirring often.

Add the cilantro and lime juice just before serving. Garnish with sour cream, scallions, and cheese, if desired. Enjoy!

Per serving: Calories 376, Protein 22 g, Fat 0 g, Carbohydrates 64 g

Tex-Mex Chili Mac

Yield: 4 servings

Invite friends and neighbors over and put some "norteno" or chicken scratch tunes on the CD player, hang a piñata, and have a fiesta! This is party food!

Combine all of the ingredients, except the cilantro, macaroni, and garnishes, in a large pot or Dutch oven. Cover and bring to a low boil. Uncover, reduce the heat to a simmer, and cook for 30 minutes, stirring often.

Add the cilantro before serving. Serve over the cooked macaroni. Garnish with cheese and scallions, if desired. Enjoy!

Per serving: Calories 568, Protein 36 g, Fat 1 g, Carbohydrates 96 g

- 2 cups beef-style textured soy granules, or 2 cups unflavored textured soy granules + ¼ cup tamari or soy sauce
- 1 medium yellow onion, chopped
- 2 green or red bell peppers, diced
- 1 carrot, diced
- 1 stalk celery, diced
- 1 (15-ounce) can crushed or diced tomatoes
- 1 (6-ounce) tomato paste
- 1 (15-ounce) can hominy
- 2 teaspoons blended chili powder
- ¼ cup canned minced jalapeño chiles
- 1 (12-ounce) bottle Mexican beer
- 2 cups cooked rattlesnake beans or kidney beans
- Salt and pepper, to taste
- 2 tablespoons minced fresh cilantro
- 1 pound corn macaroni, cooked al dente
- Grated dairy or soy cheddar cheese or Monterey Jack cheese and chopped scallions, for garnish

CHILIS!

1 tablespoon olive oil

1 large yellow onion, chopped

2 green bell peppers, diced

1 cup sliced button, shiitake, or portabella mushrooms

3 cloves garlic, minced

1 (6-ounce) can tomato paste

1 (15-ounce) can tomato sauce

2 dried ancho chiles, crushed

1 tablespoon blended chili powder

1 tablespoon ground cumin

2 cups cooked kidney or red nightfall beans

2 cups cooked navy beans

Vegetable stock or water, to cover

Salt and pepper, to taste

2 ripe avocados, diced

2 ripe mangoes, diced

Minced fresh cilantro and grated soy or dairy cheddar cheese, for garnish

JUAN'S CHILI

Yield: 6 servings

Once, at a potluck in Tucson, I enjoyed a delicious chili garnished with avocado and mango. The friend who made the dish said she got the recipe from a man named Juan. I duplicated the flavor as best I could and since then have called it Juan's Chili.

In a large pot or Dutch oven, heat the oil over medium-high heat. Add the onion and sauté until translucent, about 3 to 5 minutes.

Add the bell peppers and mushrooms, and sauté 3 minutes more. Add the garlic and sauté 1 minute more.

Add all the remaining ingredients, except the avocados, mangoes, and garnishes. Cover and bring to a boil. Uncover, reduce the heat to a simmer, and cook for 30 minutes.

Sprinkle with the avocados and mangoes before serving. Garnish with cilantro and cheese, if desired. Enjoy!

Per serving: Calories 410, Protein 13 g, Fat 11 g, Carbohydrates 63 g

Green Chile Stew
(Guisado de Chile Verde)

Yield: 4 servings

This flavorful stew has no beans, but you may add two cups of cooked pintos if you like. Serve open-faced over hot sourdough biscuits.

Heat the oil over medium-high heat in a large pot or Dutch oven. Add the onion and sauté 3 to 5 minutes, stirring frequently. Add the carrot, celery, chiles, and tomatoes, and sauté until the vegetables are somewhat tender, about 5 minutes. Add the garlic and sauté 3 minutes more.

Add all of the remaining ingredients, except the garnishes; cover and bring to a slow boil. Uncover, reduce the heat to a simmer, and cook for 30 minutes, stirring often to prevent sticking.

Serve over biscuits. Garnish with cilantro and red onion, if desired. Enjoy!

¼ cup olive oil

1 large yellow onion, chopped

1 large carrot, chopped

2 stalks celery, chopped

2 cups canned mild diced chiles

6 tomatoes, chopped

3 cloves garlic, minced

2 cups "chicken"-flavored seitan chunks

½ cup masa harina or yellow cornmeal

2 tablespoons blended chili powder

1 tablespoon tamari or soy sauce

1 tablespoon nutritional yeast

Vegetable stock or water, to cover

Salt and pepper, to taste

Minced fresh cilantro and diced red onion, for garnish

Per serving: Calories 541, Protein 46 g, Fat 14 g, Carbohydrates 57 g

- 1 medium onion, chopped
- 1 (15-ounce) can tomato purée
- 1 cup beef-style textured soy chunks, or 1 cup unflavored textured soy chunks + 2 tablespoons tamari or soy sauce
- 1 tablespoon blended chili powder
- 1 teaspoon ground cumin
- ½ teaspoon cinnamon
- ½ teaspoon dried oregano
- Pinch nutmeg
- Pinch cloves
- 2 ounces bittersweet chocolate or plain carob candy bar
- 2 fresh Anaheim chiles, roasted, peeled, and minced
- 2 cups cooked pinto or tiger eye beans
- Vegetable stock or water, to cover
- Salt and pepper, to taste
- Minced fresh cilantro, grated Monterey Jack or soy cheddar cheese, and sour cream, for garnish

CHILI MOLE

Yield: 4 servings

Hot peppers and chocolate—mole constitutes nirvana for some. Exotically different, sweet and spicy, serve this with lots of cornbread.

Combine all of the ingredients, except the garnishes, in a large pot or Dutch oven. Cover and bring to a boil over medium-high heat, stirring frequently. Uncover, reduce the heat to a low simmer, and cook for 30 minutes. Stir often to prevent sticking, adding more stock or water if it gets too thick.

Garnish with cilantro, cheese, and sour cream, if desired. Enjoy!

Per serving: Calories 327, Protein 20 g, Fat 7 g, Carbohydrates 46 g

TEXAS WHITE CHILI

Yield: 4 servings

White chili, though quite different from the traditional red, has a lot of flavor. This hearty recipe is a combination of several I've used, and I think it incorporates the best of each!

Heat the oil in a large pot or Dutch oven over medium-high heat. Add the onion and sauté until soft and translucent, about 3 to 5 minutes. Add the garlic and chiles, and sauté 2 to 3 minutes more.

Add all of the remaining ingredients, except the garnishes. Cover and bring to a low boil. Uncover, reduce the heat to a simmer, and cook 30 minutes, stirring often to prevent sticking.

Garnish with tomatoes, scallions, and cilantro, if desired. Enjoy!

Per serving: Calories 382, Protein 22 g, Fat 15 g, Carbohydrates 34 g

2 tablespoons olive oil

1 large white onion, chopped

2 cloves garlic, minced

1 (4-ounce) can mild diced chiles

1 pound firm tofu, frozen, thawed, drained, and crumbled (see Tofu Chili recipe, page 82)

¼ cup vegetarian "chicken" broth powder

1 tablespoon blended chili powder

1 teaspoon ground cumin

1 teaspoon dried oregano

1 teaspoon ground coriander

1 tablespoon nutritional yeast (see page 39)

Pinch ground cloves

Pinch cayenne

2 cups cooked navy or great Northern beans

Vegetable stock or water, to cover

Salt and pepper, to taste

½ cup grated Monterey Jack cheese

Diced tomatoes, minced scallions, and finely minced fresh cilantro, for garnish

73

¼ cup olive oil

1 large yellow onion, chopped

2 cups vegetarian sausage

4 tomatoes, chopped

1 (6-ounce) can tomato paste

1 (12-ounce) bottle Mexican beer (optional)

3 cloves garlic, minced

½ cup strong decaf or regular coffee or grain beverage

2 tablespoons blended chili powder

1 tablespoon cocoa or carob powder

1 teaspoon ground cumin

1 teaspoon oregano

½ teaspoon ground coriander

2 fresh jalapeño chiles, roasted, peeled, and minced

2 cups cooked Anasazi beans

Vegetable stock or water, to cover

Salt and pepper, to taste

Minced fresh cilantro, grated sharp cheddar cheese, and sour cream, for garnish

Sedona RedeYe Chili

Yield: 4 servings

Traditional "redeye" stew was flavored with a "secret ingredient": coffee. If you've given up coffee, substitute a grain beverage such as Cafix or Pero. Serve with blue corn muffins.

Heat the oil in a large pot or Dutch oven. Add the onion and sauté 3 to 5 minutes over medium-high heat. Add the vegetarian sausage and brown, stirring constantly, for 5 to 7 minutes.

Add all of the remaining ingredients, except the garnishes; cover and bring to a boil. Uncover, reduce the heat to a simmer, and cook for 30 minutes.

Garnish with cilantro, cheese, and sour cream, if desired. Enjoy!

Per serving: Calories 317, Protein 17 g, Fat 16 g, Carbohydrates 40 g

BLACK BEAN AND BUTTERNUT SQUASH CHILI

Yield: 6 servings

The black beans stand out nicely against the light reddish-tan of the rest of the ingredients. Serve this with a green salad or cole slaw.

In a large pot, sauté the onion, peppers, and garlic in the olive oil over medium-high heat until tender. Add the squash and zest, and cook 10 to 15 minutes. Add the cumin, chili powder, cinnamon, and cloves. Lower the heat to a simmer, and cook 5 minutes more.

Stir in the canned tomatoes, beans, chiles, stock or water, salt, pepper, and lime juice, and cook until heated through.

Serve over the cooked rice. Garnish with lime wedges, sour cream, and cilantro, if desired. Enjoy!

Per serving: Calories 362, Protein 12 g, Fat 4 g, Carbohydrates 70 g

1 large yellow onion, diced

2 red or green bell peppers, diced

5 cloves garlic, minced

1 tablespoon olive oil

1 butternut squash, peeled and chopped into ½-inch cubes

Zest of 1 lime, minced

2 tablespoons ground cumin

1 tablespoon blended chili powder

⅛ teaspoon cinnamon

⅛ teaspoon ground cloves

2 (16-ounce) cans chopped tomatoes

3 cups cooked black beans

2 fresh chipotle chiles, roasted, peeled, and diced

Vegetable stock or water, to cover

Salt and pepper, to taste

Juice of 1 lime

4 cups cooked brown or basmati rice

Lime wedges, sour cream, and chopped fresh cilantro, for garnish

CHILIS WITH A SLIGHT TWIST

Corn–Bulgur Chili • 79
Sun–Dried Tomato Chili • 80
Mango Chili • 81
Tofu Chili • 82
Seitan Chili • 83
Tempeh Chili • 84
Amaranth Chili • 85
Spicy Autumn Harvest Chili • 86
Lentil Chili • 87
Acorn Squash Chili • 88
Midwestern Butter Bean Chili • 89
Roasted Vegetable Chili • 90
Hearty Barley Chili • 92

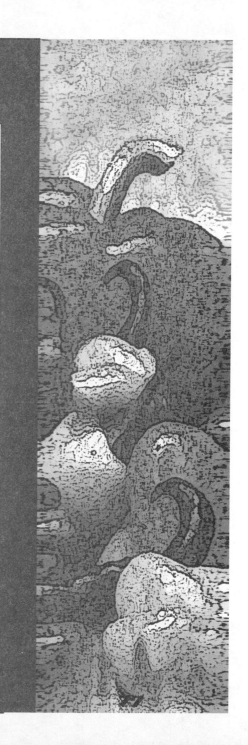

CORN-BULGUR CHILI

Yield: 4 servings

Bulgur adds a hearty, chewy texture, and the corn compliments it well. Don't forget the hot corn tortillas.

In a small saucepan, heat the tomato juice to boiling, and stir in the bulgur. Remove from the heat, cover, and let stand until the juice is absorbed, about 30 minutes. Set aside.

Combine all of the remaining ingredients, except the garnishes, in a large pot or Dutch oven. Cook over medium heat, stirring frequently, until the vegetables are tender, about 30 minutes. Stir in the bulgur mixture, and heat through.

Garnish with cilantro and olives, if desired. Enjoy!

½ cup tomato juice
½ cup uncooked bulgur
1 large onion, chopped
1 green bell pepper, chopped
2 cloves garlic, chopped
4 tomatoes, chopped
1 cup fresh or frozen corn
1½ teaspoons blended chili powder
¼ teaspoon dried oregano
½ teaspoon ground cumin
1 dried Santa Fe grande chile, crumbled
2 cups cooked soldier or kidney beans
Vegetable stock or water, to cover
Salt and pepper, to taste
Minced fresh cilantro and chopped black olives, for garnish

Per serving: Calories 278, Protein 12 g, Fat 1 g, Carbohydrates 55 g

1 red onion, chopped

1 zucchini, diced

1 green bell pepper, diced

1 cup burgundy wine (optional)

Vegetable stock, to cover

2 cloves garlic, minced

2 dried pasilla chiles, crushed

1 teaspoon ground cumin

1 teaspoon blended chili powder

½ teaspoon dried oregano

½ teaspoon dried basil

2 cups cooked scarlet runner or small red beans

½ cup sun-dried tomatoes, chopped

Salt and pepper, to taste

SUN-DRIED TOMATO CHILI

Yield: 4 servings

The smoky-sweet flavor of the pasilla peppers really enhances the richness of the sun-dried tomatoes. Serve with hot, crusty French bread and a little grated Asiago cheese. Very hearty and satisfying! Try this also chili mac-style, that is, over pasta or macaroni.

In a large pot or Dutch oven, add the onion, zucchini, and bell pepper with about ½ cup of the wine or stock. Cover and cook over medium-high heat for about 10 minutes, stirring frequently.

Add all of the remaining ingredients, and bring to a boil. Cover, reduce the heat to a low simmer, and cook 25 to 30 minutes more, stirring often. Enjoy!

Per serving: Calories 187, Protein 9 g, Fat 0 g, Carbohydrates 37 g

MANGO CHILI

Yield: 4 servings

You'll go for this spicy sweet chili. Great at a party with lots of tortilla chips!

In a large pot or Dutch oven, sauté the onion in the oil over medium heat until tender. Add the garlic and continue to sauté for 2 minutes more.

Add all of the remaining ingredients, except the cilantro and garnishes, and bring to a simmer. Reduce the heat to low, and cook, uncovered, 20 to 30 minutes, stirring often.

Add the cilantro just before serving. Garnish with scallions and cheese, if desired. Enjoy!

1 red onion, chopped

1 tablespoon toasted sesame oil

2 cloves garlic, minced

2 mangoes, peeled, seeded, and chopped

¼ cup sun-dried tomatoes, chopped

1 (15-ounce) can tomato sauce

½ teaspoon aji Amarillo chili powder

1 teaspoon ground cumin

1 teaspoon fresh ginger juice

1 cup fresh or frozen corn

2 cups cooked Colorado River or pinto beans

1 cup vegetable juice (such as V-8)

Vegetable stock, to cover

Salt and pepper, to taste

¼ cup minced fresh cilantro

Chopped scallions, and grated goat cheese, for garnish

Per serving: Calories 315, Protein 9 g, Fat 5 g, Carbohydrates 59 g

1 tablespoon toasted sesame oil

2 tablespoons tamari or soy sauce

Juice of 1 lime

1 teaspoon rice vinegar

1 red onion, chopped

1 small zucchini, diced

4 tomatoes, chopped

4 to 6 shiitake mushrooms, sliced

3 cloves garlic, minced

1 pound firm tofu, frozen, thawed, drained, and crumbled

1 teaspoon blended chili powder

1 teaspoon crushed red pepper flakes

½ teaspoon curry powder

Vegetable stock or water, to cover

1 (6-ounce) can tomato paste

2 cups cooked adzuki beans

Salt and pepper, to taste

2 cups cooked basmati rice

Minced fresh cilantro and chopped spring onions, for garnish

TOFU CHILI

Yield: 4 servings

Though tofu has little flavor of its own, it readily takes on whatever flavors it is mixed with. Freezing tofu changes its texture and, when defrosted and crumbled, it resembles ground beef but lighter.

In a large pot or Dutch oven, combine the oil, tamari, lime juice, and vinegar. Add the onion, zucchini, tomatoes, and mushrooms, and sauté 3 to 5 minutes over medium-high heat, stirring frequently.

Add the garlic and sauté 1 or 2 minutes more. Add the tofu and spices and ⅓ cup of the stock or water. Cover and steam for 5 minutes, stirring occasionally to keep it from sticking.

Add the remaining stock or water, the tomato paste, beans, and salt and pepper. Bring to a low boil. Reduce the heat to a simmer and cook, uncovered, at least 20 minutes more. Serve over the cooked rice. Garnish with cilantro and onions, if desired. Enjoy!

Per serving: Calories 473, Protein 22 g, Fat 9 g, Carbohydrates 74 g

Seitan Chili

Yield: 4 servings

Though used for centuries in Japan and other Asian countries, seitan, also called wheat gluten or wheat meat, is fairly new to Americans. The texture is nicely chewy but tender, and it really makes a nice addition to stews and chilis. Serve with whole-grain crackers or tortilla chips.

In a large pot or Dutch oven, sauté the onion in the oil for 2 or 3 minutes over medium-high heat.

Add the mushrooms, bell pepper, and tomatoes, and cook for 2 to 3 minutes more. Add the garlic and cook 1 minute more.

Add all of the remaining ingredients, except the garnishes; cover and bring to a boil. Remove the cover, reduce the heat to a simmer, and cook 25 to 30 minutes more, stirring often.

Garnish with cilantro and cheese, if desired. Enjoy!

Per serving: Calories 486, Protein 45 g, Fat 7 g, Carbohydrates 59 g

Chilis With A Slight Twist

- 1 medium yellow onion, chopped
- 2 tablespoons olive oil
- 1 cup button mushrooms, sliced
- 1 green bell pepper, diced
- 4 tomatoes, chopped
- 2 cloves garlic, minced
- 2 cups "chicken"-flavored seitan, chopped
- 2 tablespoons minced canned jalapeño chiles
- 1 teaspoon chipotle chili powder
- 2 cups cooked pinto or kidney beans
- Tomato juice, to cover
- Salt and pepper, to taste
- Minced fresh cilantro and cheese of your choice, for garnish

1 tablespoon hot sesame oil

1 tablespoon tamari or soy sauce

Vegetable stock or water, to cover (see variation below instructions)

1 medium yellow onion, chopped

1 cup sliced mushrooms

1 red bell pepper, diced

6 tomatoes, chopped

2 cloves garlic, minced

2 (8-ounce) packages five-grain tempeh, finely chopped

1 dried chipotle chile, crushed

1 teaspoon blended chili powder

1 teaspoon ground cumin

Pinch each cinnamon and cloves

¼ cup minced fresh cilantro

½ cup roasted whole peanuts

Salt and pepper, to taste

Sour cream and grated sharp cheddar cheese, for garnish

TEMPEH CHILI

Yield: 4 servings

Like tofu, tempeh is an Asian staple made from soybeans. Tempeh—cakes of fermented soybeans—has a stronger flavor and chewier texture than tofu. It comes in several flavors and makes a hearty, tasty addition to this spicy chili. I did not include beans in this recipe, but if you like, you might add some adzuki or black beans.

In a large pot or Dutch oven, combine the oil and tamari with 2 tablespoons of the stock or water. Add the onion and sauté over medium-high heat until tender, about 2 to 3 minutes. Add the mushrooms, bell pepper, and tomatoes, and cook 3 to 5 minutes more, stirring often. Add the garlic and cook another minute or so.

Add all of the remaining ingredients, except the garnishes, and bring to a low boil. Reduce the heat to a simmer, and cook, uncovered, 25 to 30 minutes. Garnish with sour cream and cheese, if desired. Enjoy!

Variation: For a different, yet quite interesting flavor, substitute ½ cup orange juice for an equal amount of the vegetable stock.

Per serving: Calories 423, Protein 25 g, Fat 19 g, Carbohydrates 35 g

AMARANTH CHILI

Yield: 4 servings

Amaranth, a highly nutritious grain cultivated by the Aztecs, grows quite well and beautifully in many gardens. It is also available in any health food store and is well worth experimenting with. I came across a variation of this recipe some time back and played with it until this tasty stew resulted. Serve with lots of crackers or tortilla chips.

Combine all of the ingredients, except the cilantro and garnishes, in a large pot or Dutch oven; cover and bring to a low boil. Uncover, reduce the heat to a simmer, and cook for 20 minutes, stirring frequently. If it becomes too thick, add more water or stock.

Add the cilantro just before serving. Garnish with tomato and onion if desired. Enjoy!

Per serving: Calories 344, Protein 15 g, Fat 3 g, Carbohydrates 65 g

2 cups cooked amaranth

1 red bell pepper, diced

3 tomatoes, chopped

1 yellow onion, chopped

2 cloves garlic, minced

1 (4-ounce) can mild chiles, diced

1 dried chipotle chile, crushed

1 tablespoon blended chili powder

1 teaspoon ground cumin

2 cups cooked anasazi beans

Vegetable stock or water, to cover

Salt and pepper, to taste

¼ cup minced fresh cilantro

Diced tomato and diced onion, for garnish

- 1 cup diced butternut or acorn squash
- 1 cup diced sweet potatoes
- 2 carrots, diced
- 1 medium yellow onion, chopped
- 6 tomatoes, chopped
- 2 unpeeled apples, diced
- Juice of 1 lemon
- 1 tablespoon blended chili powder
- ½ teaspoon cinnamon
- ½ teaspoon curry powder
- 2 cups cooked garbanzo beans
- 2 fresh jalapeño chiles, roasted, peeled, and minced
- 1 cup vegetable juice (such as V-8)
- Vegetable stock, to cover
- Salt and pepper, to taste
- Sour cream, for garnish

SPICY AUTUMN HARVEST CHILI

Yield: 4 servings

Similar to mulligatawny, this chili is a delicious way to use those autumn vegetables. Throw a big harvest party, and serve this as the main course with dark brown bread or corn muffins. Don't forget to freeze some for those cold winter nights.

Combine all the ingredients, except the sour cream, in a large pot or Dutch oven. Cover and bring to a slow boil. Uncover, reduce the heat to a low simmer, and cook, stirring often, for 40 minutes.

Garnish with sour cream, if desired. Enjoy!

Per serving: Calories 323, Protein 10 g, Fat 1 g, Carbohydrates 65 g

LeNTiL CHiLi

Yield: 4 servings

Lentils have a "beefy" flavor and replace the more traditional pinto or kidney beans well in this thick chili. They also cook quite a bit faster (no need to soak them either), so this makes a good recipe when you're rushed for time.

In a large pot or Dutch oven, combine the oil with ¼ cup of the stock or water and the tamari over medium-high heat. Add the onion and sauté until translucent, about 3 to 5 minutes.

Add the bell pepper, carrots, celery, and tomatoes, and cook 5 minutes. Add the garlic and sauté 1 minute.

Add all of the remaining ingredients, except the garnishes. Cover and bring to a boil. Uncover, reduce the heat to a simmer, and cook for 30 minutes.

Garnish with cilantro and cheese, if desired. Enjoy!

Per serving: Calories 286, Protein 11 g, Fat 2 g, Carbohydrates 53 g

2 teaspoons toasted sesame oil

Vegetable stock or water, to cover + ¼ cup

1 tablespoon tamari or soy sauce

1 medium onion, chopped

1 green bell pepper, diced

2 small carrots, diced

1 stalk celery, diced

4 tomatoes, chopped

2 small red unpeeled potatoes, chopped

2 cloves garlic, minced

¼ cup masa harina or cornmeal

1 fresh poblano chile, roasted, peeled, and diced

1 tablespoon blended chili powder

2 cups cooked green or brown lentils

Salt and pepper, to taste

Minced fresh cilantro and grated pepper-Jack cheese, for garnish

1 medium yellow onion, chopped

2 red bell peppers, diced

1 large or 2 small acorn or other winter squash, peeled and chopped

1 cup fresh or frozen corn

2 tablespoons blended chili powder

1 tablespoon ground cumin

1 teaspoon oregano

¼ teaspoon allspice

1 dried poblano chile, crushed

1 tablespoon minced orange zest

7 or 8 plum tomatoes, chopped

½ cup dry red wine (Burgundy or Chianti)

1 cup cooked red kidney beans

1 cup cooked black beans

Vegetable stock or water, to cover

Salt and pepper, to taste

⅓ cup minced fresh cilantro

Grated soy or dairy cheddar cheese and chopped scallions, for garnish

ACORN SQUASH CHILI

Yield: 4 servings

This colorful stew is always a big hit at potlucks and parties, as well as a tasty way to use all those winter squash from the garden! Serve it with blue corn muffins and a green salad.

Combine all of the ingredients, except the cilantro and garnishes, in a large pot or Dutch oven. Cover and bring to a boil, stirring often. Uncover, reduce the heat to a simmer, and cook for 30 minutes.

Add the cilantro before serving. Garnish with cheese and scallions, if desired. Enjoy!

Per serving: Calories 275, Protein 10 g, Fat 1 g, Carbohydrates 48 g

MidWestern Butter Bean Chili

Yield: 4 servings

This is a good chili for those who are novices to the delights of a good "bowl o' red." If you are really unused to spicy foods, use only half of the poblano chile and omit the cayenne. Serve with whole grain crackers or bread.

Combine all of the ingredients, except the garnishes, in a large pot or Dutch oven; cover and bring to a boil. Uncover, reduce the heat to a simmer, and cook for 30 minutes.

Garnish with cilantro, cheese, and sour cream, if desired. Enjoy!

Per serving: Calories 223, Protein 18 g, Fat 0 g, Carbohydrates 36 g

Chilis With A Slight Twist

- 1 cup chicken-style textured soy chunks, or 1 cup unflavored soy chunks + 1 teaspoon vegetarian "chicken" broth powder
- 1 medium yellow onion, chopped
- 4 tomatoes, chopped
- 3 cloves garlic, minced
- 1 fresh poblano chile, roasted, peeled, and minced
- ½ teaspoon dried basil
- Pinch allspice
- Pinch cayenne
- 2 cups cooked butter beans (limas)
- Vegetable stock or water, to cover
- Salt and pepper, to taste
- Minced fresh cilantro, cheddar cheese, and sour cream, for garnish

¼ cup olive oil

3 cloves garlic, minced

1 tablespoon balsamic vinegar

1 teaspoon liquid smoke (optional)

3 fresh Anaheim chiles, chopped

1 red bell pepper, roughly chopped

1 large zucchini, cut into thick slices

2 small eggplants, cut into thick slices

2 large beefsteak tomatoes, cut into thick slices

20 large button mushrooms, stems removed

2 medium yellow onions, quartered; quarters held together with toothpicks

2 cups cooked large kidney beans

1 tablespoon blended chili powder

Pinch crushed red pepper flakes

ROASTED VEGETABLE CHILI

Yield: 4 servings

Roasted vegetables add another delicious dimension to this flavorful dish. Serve it for a special occasion and don't call it chili— that seems too mundane for such a combination of flavors. Don't forget the homemade cornbread.

To make the marinade for the vegetables, mix together the oil, garlic, vinegar, and liquid smoke, if desired, in a small bowl.

Place the chiles, bell pepper, zucchini, eggplant, tomatoes, mushrooms, and onions in a shallow baking dish, and cover with half of the marinade, reserving the rest for basting. Refrigerate the marinating vegetables for at least 2 hours.

Prepare a gas or charcoal grill. When hot, gently grill the vegetables about 5 to 10 minutes per side, basting with the marinade. Remove the vegetables from the grill, and set aside until they are cool enough to handle.

Chop the roasted vegetables, peel the chiles, and combine them with all of the remaining ingredients, except the garnishes, in a large pot. Cover and bring to a boil. Uncover, reduce the heat to a simmer, and cook for 30 minutes.

Garnish with cilantro and cheese, if desired. Enjoy!

2 teaspoons ground cumin
Pinch dried oregano
Vegetable stock, to cover
Salt and pepper, to taste
Minced fresh cilantro and grated Asiago cheese, for garnish

Per serving: Calories 343, Protein 11 g, Fat 14 g, Carbohydrates 42 g

1/3 cup uncooked barley

1 medium onion, chopped

1 green bell pepper, chopped

3 tomatoes, chopped

4 cloves garlic, minced

1 canned whole jalapeño chile, chopped

1 tablespoon blended chili powder

2 cups cooked red or kidney beans

1/3 cup minced fresh cilantro

Vegetable stock or water, to cover

Salt and pepper, to taste

Grated Monterey Jack cheese and chopped scallions, for garnish

Hearty Barley Chili

Yield: 4 servings

Barley adds a hearty texture and a sweet flavor that compliments this chili quite well. Cornbread would make a nice accompaniment.

Combine all the ingredients, except the garnishes, in a large pot or Dutch oven. Bring to a boil and reduce the heat to a medium simmer. Cover and cook 1 hour. Stir occasionally to keep it from sticking on the bottom, and add a little vegetable stock or water if it gets too dry or thick.

If you used a crock pot to cook the beans, you might just want to combine the rest of the ingredients with the beans. It will take a little longer to cook, but the advantage is that you can leave it unattended for a long period of time. Cook on high, covered, for 2 to 3 hours.

Garnish with cheese and scallions, if desired. Enjoy!

Per serving: Calories 191, Protein 9 g, Fat 0 g, Carbohydrates 37 g

CHILIS WITH A BIG TWIST

Macrobiotic Chili • 95

Artichoke Chili • 96

California Chili • 97

Three-Mushroom Chili with Sour
    Cherries • 98

Cape Cod Cranberry-Tofu Chili • 100

Savory Apricot Chili • 101

Peanut Chili Mole • 102

Cashew and Raisin Chili • 103

Georgia Sweet Potato Chili • 104

MACROBIOTIC CHILI

Yield: 4 servings

With no tomatoes and only the slightest hint of hot chiles, this tasty stew stretches the definition of "chili" just a bit, but don't let that worry you. It's still delicious and hearty, no matter what you might call it.

In a large wok or skillet, heat the oil, vinegar, and ¼ cup of the stock over medium-high heat. Add the onion and sauté lightly for about 2 minutes. Add the zucchini, mushrooms, and carrots, cover and cook, stirring often, until the vegetables are crunchy-tender (about 3 minutes).

Dissolve the arrowroot powder in the remaining ¼ cup of vegetable stock, and add to the vegetables along with the tamari, red pepper flakes, and beans. Cook, stirring often, until heated through, adding vegetable juice as needed to keep it from becoming too thick.

Serve over the cooked brown rice. Garnish with scallions and gomasio, if desired. Enjoy!

½ teaspoon hot sesame oil

1 teaspoon brown rice vinegar

½ cup vegetable stock

1 medium yellow onion, chopped

2 zucchini, sliced in half lengthwise, then sliced crosswise on the diagonal into half-moons

1 cup sliced shiitake mushrooms

2 carrots, cut into julienne

¼ cup arrowroot powder

Tamari or soy sauce, to taste

Pinch crushed red pepper flakes, or to taste

2 cups cooked adzuki beans

½ cup tomato-less vegetable juice

4 cups cooked short-grain brown rice

Chopped scallions and gomasio, for garnish

Per serving: Calories 474, Protein 15 g, Fat 2 g, Carbohydrates 99 g

1 (5-ounce) jar marinated artichoke hearts, drained and chopped, oil and liquid reserved

1 medium red onion, chopped

1 red or green bell pepper, diced

4 tomatoes, chopped

3 cloves garlic, minced

1 tablespoon blended chili powder

1 teaspoon ground cumin

1 teaspoon dried oregano

1 teaspoon dried basil

1 fresh Anaheim chile, roasted, peeled, and minced

1 fresh pasilla chile, roasted, peeled, and minced

2 cups cooked navy beans

Vegetable stock or water, to cover

Salt and pepper, to taste

Crumbled feta or goat cheese, minced fresh cilantro, and chopped olives, for garnish

ARTICHOKE CHILI

Yield: 4 servings

I've always liked artichoke hearts in pasta sauce, and one day I thought, "Why not try some in my chili?" Why not indeed? They're delicious in chili. I hope you think so too.

Heat the reserved oil and liquid from the drained artichoke hearts in a large pot or Dutch oven over medium-high heat. Add the onion and sauté until translucent, about 3 to 5 minutes. Add the bell pepper and tomatoes, and cook 3 to 5 minutes. Add the garlic and cook 1 minute more.

Add all of the remaining ingredients, except the garnishes; cover and bring to a boil. Reduce the heat to a simmer and cook, uncovered, for 30 minutes.

Garnish with cheese, cilantro, and olives, if desired. Enjoy!

Per serving: Calories 197, Protein 9 g, Fat 0 g, Carbohydrates 38 g

CALIFORNIA CHILI

Yield: 4 servings

One thing I've always liked about California chefs is their willingness to experiment. Who's to say artichoke hearts, balsamic vinegar, or kalamata olives won't taste good together in chili? Not me! Though not quite traditional, this is delicious.

Combine all of the ingredients, except the garnishes, in a large pot or Dutch oven. Cover and bring to a low boil. Remove the cover, reduce the heat to a simmer, and cook for 30 minutes, stirring often.

Garnish with olives and cheese, if desired. Enjoy!

Per serving: Calories 239, Protein 10 g, Fat 0 g, Carbohydrates 44 g

1 red onion, chopped

½ cup chopped sun-dried tomatoes

1 cup marinated artichoke hearts, drained and chopped

1 tablespoon balsamic vinegar

½ cup chopped fresh basil

2 dried chipotle chiles, crushed

2 cups cooked adzuki or black beans

½ cup red wine (Burgundy, Chianti, etc.)

Vegetable juice (such as V-8), to cover

Salt and pepper, to taste

6 kalamata olives and crumbled Asiago or feta cheese, for garnish

2 tablespoons toasted sesame oil

1 large onion, chopped

1 pound shiitake mushrooms, sliced

1 pound chanterelles or oyster mushrooms, chopped

1 pound button mushrooms, sliced

1 large green bell pepper, diced

3 cloves garlic, minced

1 teaspoon tamari or soy sauce

2 cups tomato juice

1 cup orange juice

6 tomatoes, chopped

1 cup fresh or frozen corn

1 fresh chipotle chile, roasted, peeled, and minced

1 ancho chile, roasted, peeled, and minced

THREE-MUSHROOM CHILI WITH SOUR CHERRIES

Yield: 6 servings

All right. I admit this one sounds pretty strange—mushrooms, cherries, orange juice, corn—but put your skepticism aside, and try it. This is not just unusual, but unusually good!

Heat the oil over medium-high heat in a large pot or Dutch oven, and gently sauté the onion and mushrooms about 5 minutes, stirring often.

Add the bell pepper and garlic, and sauté 3 to 5 minutes more.

Add all of the remaining ingredients, except the garnishes; cover and bring to a slow boil.

1 cup dried sour cherries

1 teaspoon blended chili powder

1 tablespoon ground cumin

2 cups cooked black turtle beans

Salt and pepper, to taste

Minced fresh cilantro, chopped scallions, and crumbled goat cheese, for garnish

Uncover, reduce the heat to a simmer, and cook 30 minutes.

Garnish with cilantro, scallions, and goat cheese, if desired. Enjoy!

Per serving: Calories 324, Protein 10 g, Fat 5 g, Carbohydrates 57 g

2 tablespoons olive oil

1 medium red onion, chopped

1 pound firm tofu, drained and crumbled

4 tomatoes, chopped

1 stalk celery, diced

2 fresh jalapeño chiles, roasted, peeled, and minced

3 cloves garlic, minced

½ cup fresh or frozen cranberries

1 tablespoon tamari or soy sauce

2 tablespoons blended chili powder

¼ cup vegetarian "chicken" broth powder

Pinch cinnamon

Salt and pepper, to taste

2 cups cooked soldier or kidney beans

Juice of 1 lime

Vegetable stock or water, to cover

¼ cup minced fresh cilantro

¼ cup nutritional yeast

Sour cream and chopped scallions, for garnish

CAPE COD CRANBERRY-TOFU CHILI

Yield: 4 servings

Here's another recipe that could compete in a "most unusual" category at a chili cook-off, but don't let that bother you—this is a very tasty chili!

Heat the oil over medium-high heat in a large pot or Dutch oven. Add the onion and tofu, and sauté, stirring constantly, until the tofu is lightly browned and the onion is tender, about 5 minutes.

Add the tomatoes, celery, chiles, garlic, cranberries and tamari, and cook 5 minutes more, stirring constantly. Add the chili powder, broth powder, cinnamon, salt, and pepper; cook 5 minutes, stirring constantly.

Add the beans, lime juice, and stock or water. Bring to a boil, reduce the heat to a simmer, and cook for 30 minutes, stirring often.

Stir in the cilantro and nutritional yeast just before serving. Garnish with sour cream and scallions, if desired. Enjoy!

Per serving: Calories 412, Protein 25 g, Fat 14 g, Carbohydrates 40 g

SAVORY APRICOT CHILI

Yield: 4 servings

Dried apricots add a nicely subtle sweetness and rich texture to this recipe. Serve with corn muffins.

Combine all of the ingredients, except the garnishes, in a large pot or Dutch oven. Cover and bring to a boil over medium-high heat. Uncover, reduce the heat to a simmer, and cook for 30 minutes, stirring often.

Garnish with cilantro and onion, if desired.

* For the beef-style textured soy chunks, you can substitute 1 cup textured soy chunks + 2 tablespoons tamari or soy sauce.

1 cup beef-style textured soy chunks*

1 large yellow onion, chopped

1 green bell pepper, diced

3 cloves garlic, minced

1 fresh Santa Fe grande chile, roasted, peeled, and minced

8 unsulphured dried apricots, chopped

2 tablespoons blended chili powder

1 teaspoon ground cumin

1 teaspoon dried oregano

Pinch cayenne (optional)

¼ cup masa harina or cornmeal

1 teaspoon Barbados or mild molasses

1 (12-ounce) bottle Mexican beer (optional)

1 teaspoon prepared mustard, any type

1 (15-ounce) can tomato sauce

1 (6-ounce) can tomato paste

Vegetable stock or water, to cover

Salt and pepper, to taste

Minced fresh cilantro and chopped red onion, for garnish

Per serving: Calories 220, Protein 14 g, Fat 0 g, Carbohydrates 38 g

1 cup beef-style textured soy chunks*

1 medium yellow onion, chopped

½ pound button mushrooms, sliced

6 fresh tomatoes, chopped

3 cloves garlic, minced

1 (16-ounce) can tomato purée

1 tablespoon blended chili powder

1 dried serrano chile, crushed

1 teaspoon cinnamon

Pinch cloves

2 heaping tablespoons crunchy peanut butter

2 squares baking chocolate, or ¼ cup carob chips

2 cups cooked kidney or pinto beans

Vegetable stock or water, to cover

Salt and pepper, to taste

Minced fresh cilantro and chopped scallions, for garnish

Peanut Chili Mole

Yield: 4 servings

This is somewhat like the other mole recipe on page 72, but I've taken the liberty of adding a little peanut butter. Yum!

Combine all of the ingredients, except the garnishes, in a large pot or Dutch oven. Cover and bring to a boil over medium-high heat. Remove the cover and cook 30 minutes, stirring often.

Garnish with cilantro and scallions, if desired. Enjoy!

* For the beef-style textured soy chunks, you can substitute 1 cup textured soy chunks + 2 tablespoons tamari or soy sauce.

Per serving: Calories 419, Protein 25 g, Fat 11 g, Carbohydrates 55 g

CASHEW AND RAISIN CHILI

Yield: 4 servings

Cashews and raisins might sound a little odd for a chili, but once you've tried this, it's sure to become a favorite. Serve this with cornbread or pita bread and a garden salad or coleslaw on the side.

Combine all of the ingredients, except the garnishes, in a large pot or Dutch oven, and bring to a slow boil. Cover, reduce the heat to low, and cook for 40 minutes.

Garnish with olives and cheese, if desired. Enjoy!

1 medium onion, chopped

1 green bell pepper, chopped

2 stalks celery, chopped

2 cups fresh or frozen corn

6 tomatoes, chopped

1 dried costeno Amarillo chile, crushed

1 clove garlic, minced

1 tablespoon blended chili powder

1 teaspoon ground cumin

1 teaspoon dried basil

1 teaspoon dried oregano

½ teaspoon black pepper

1 bay leaf

2 cups cooked red or kidney beans

1 cup raisins

1 cup cashews

1 cup vegetable juice (such as V-8)

Salt and pepper, to taste

Chopped olives and feta cheese, for garnish

Per serving: Calories 572, Protein 16 g, Fat 17 g, Carbohydrates 88 g

1 large yellow onion, chopped

1 green bell pepper, diced

4 tomatoes, chopped

2 medium sweet potatoes, peeled and diced

2 cloves garlic, minced

1 cup fresh or frozen corn

¼ cup barbecue sauce

1 dried chipotle chile, crushed

2 tablespoons blended chili powder

½ teaspoon cinnamon

Pinch nutmeg

Pinch crushed red pepper flakes

2 cups cooked black-eyed peas or speckled brown cow beans

1 teaspoon liquid smoke (optional)

Vegetable stock or water, to cover

Salt and pepper, to taste

Minced fresh parsley and cilantro, for garnish

GEORGIA SWEET POTATO CHILI

Yield: 4 servings

This is another recipe I thought sounded strange but intriguing. I was delightfully surprised at how quickly it became a favorite of my "test crew." I think your family will like it just as much. It's great with fresh cornbread.

Combine all of the ingredients, except the garnishes, in a large pot or Dutch oven. Cover and bring to a slow boil over medium-high heat.

Uncover, reduce the heat to a simmer, and cook for 30 minutes, stirring often.

Garnish with parsley and cilantro, if desired. Enjoy!

Per serving: Calories 275, Protein 9 g, Fat 0 g, Carbohydrates 58 g

CHILIS AROUND THE WORLD

Caribbean Chili • 107

Thai Chili • 108

Shiitake and Portabella Mushroom Chili • 109

Black Bean and Corn Chili with Polenta • 110

Hawaiian Chili • 112

Ethiopian Chili • 113

Pesto Chili • 114

Rat-a-tat Chili • 115

Hungarian Goulash Chili • 116

Beet-Sour Cream Chili • 117

Mediterranean Chili • 118

CARIBBEAN CHILI

Yield: 4 servings

Hot chile peppers abound in the Caribbean, including some of the hottest— habañeros and Scotch bonnets. If your tolerance of hot, spicy foods runs to the mild side, substitute something less incendiary, like Anaheim chiles.

Combine all of the ingredients, except the cilantro and garnishes, in a large pot or Dutch oven; cover and bring to a low boil. Uncover, reduce the heat to a simmer, and cook for 40 minutes, stirring frequently.

Add the cilantro just before serving. Garnish with sour cream and citrus zest, if desired. Enjoy!

Per serving: Calories 267, Protein 11 g, Fat 1 g, Carbohydrates 53 g

6 tomatoes, chopped

1 medium yellow onion, chopped

1 cup fresh chopped pineapple or canned unsweetened pineapple chunks

Juice of 1 orange

Juice of 1 lime

1 red or green bell pepper, chopped

2 cloves garlic, minced

1 tablespoon blended chili powder

1 teaspoon ground cumin

⅛ teaspoon or less crushed dried habañero or Scotch bonnet chile

3 cups cooked black beans

1 cup tomato juice

Vegetable stock or water, to cover

Salt and pepper, to taste

⅓ cup minced fresh cilantro

Sour cream, and orange and lime zest, for garnish

1 tablespoon hot sesame oil

Juice of 2 limes

Vegetable juice or stock, to cover + ¼ cup

3 scallions, chopped

3 tomatoes, chopped

2 carrots, cut into matchsticks

½ cup sliced button or shiitake mushrooms

1 red bell pepper, cut into julienne strips

1 cup finely shredded cabbage or bok choy

3 cloves garlic, minced

½ cup tomato sauce

2 tablespoons peanut butter

½ teaspoon Thai chile sauce

Tamari or soy sauce, to taste

2 cups cooked Christmas or kidney beans

4 cups cooked jasmine rice

Minced fresh cilantro and tamari-roasted cashews, for garnish

THAI CHILI

Yield: 4 servings

Outside of the Caribbean, Thailand grows some of the hottest chiles available on the market. Their chile sauces are especially flavorful and add a lot of zip to this Asian-style chili. Serve some on the side as well, so people can add a little "heat."

In a large pot or wok, combine the oil, lime juice, and ¼ cup of the stock or water. Over medium-high heat, steam the scallions, tomatoes, carrots, mushrooms, and bell pepper about 5 minutes, stirring often and covering the pot between stirrings.

Add the cabbage or bok choy and garlic, and cook for 2 to 3 minutes more.

Add the tomato sauce, peanut butter, chile sauce, tamari, and beans. Reduce the heat to a simmer, cover, and cook 5 to 7 minutes more.

Serve over the cooked rice. Garnish with cilantro and cashews, if desired. Enjoy!

Per serving: Calories 448, Protein 14 g, Fat 7 g, Carbohydrates 78 g

SHIITAKE AND PORTABELLA MUSHROOM CHILI

Yield: 4 servings

With its peanut butter, lime juice, and Thai chili paste, this chili seems more in the spirit of Thai food. Try this served over soba or udon noodles, perhaps. It's also quite tasty served open-faced over biscuits.

Place the oil, red pepper flakes, vinegar, and 1 tablespoon of the stock in a large skillet or wok. Add the onion and sauté over medium-high heat for 3 to 5 minutes, stirring often.

Add the mushrooms, bell pepper, and tomatoes, and cook 2 to 3 minutes more. Add the garlic and cook 2 minutes.

Add the chile paste, if desired, beans, peanut butter, lime juice, and tamari; cook, uncovered, over medium heat, until bubbly and beginning to thicken, about 10 to 15 minutes. Stir often to keep it from sticking or scorching.

Serve over the hot cooked rice. Garnish with scallions and cilantro, if desired. Enjoy!

Per serving: Calories 429, Protein 16 g, Fat 5 g, Carbohydrates 79 g

½ teaspoon hot sesame oil

¼ teaspoon crushed red pepper flakes

1 teaspoon balsamic vinegar

Vegetable stock, to cover

1 medium yellow onion, chopped

2 cups sliced shiitake and portabella mushrooms

1 red bell pepper, cut in julienne

2 tomatoes, chopped

2 cloves garlic, minced

Pinch Thai or Korean chile paste (optional)

2 cups cooked adzuki beans

2 tablespoons peanut butter

Juice of 1 lime

Tamari or soy sauce, to taste

3 cups cooked brown or basmati rice

Chopped scallions and minced fresh cilantro, for garnish

2¼ cups water

¾ cup yellow cornmeal

¾ cup cold water

Salt, to taste

1 medium onion, chopped

2 cloves garlic, minced

2 fresh jalapeño chiles, roasted, peeled, and chopped

1 tablespoon olive oil

1 teaspoon dried oregano

¾ teaspoon ground cumin

1 (14-ounce) can Mexican-style stewed tomatoes, drained; liquid reserved

1 (8-ounce) can tomato sauce

1 (12-ounce) bottle Mexican beer

2 cups cooked black beans

1 cup frozen corn

Black pepper, to taste

1 cup crumbled goat cheese and minced, fresh cilantro, for garnish

BLACK BEAN AND CORN CHILI WITH POLENTA

Yield: 4 servings

This makes an especially hearty meal, quite colorful and attractive. Serve this for a special occasion or when "company's comin'." Though polenta is of Italian origin, it lends itself very well to Southwestern dishes.

To make the polenta, bring the 2¼ cups water to a boil in a medium saucepan. In a small bowl, combine the cornmeal, the ¾ cup cold water, and salt. Slowly add the cornmeal mixture to the boiling water, stirring constantly. Cook and stir until the mixture returns to a boil. Reduce the heat to very low. Cover and simmer for 15 minutes, stirring occasionally.

Pour the hot polenta mixture into an oiled, 8 x 8 x 2-inch baking pan. Cool for 1 hour at room temperature. Cover with plastic wrap and chill until firm, several hours or overnight.

Sauté the onion, garlic, and fresh jalapeño in the oil in a saucepan over medium heat until tender

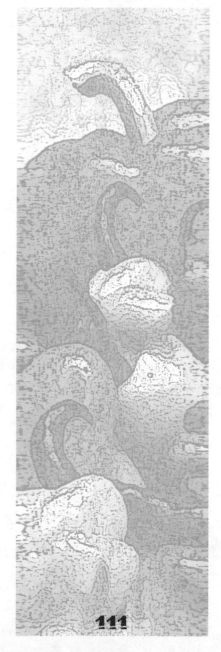

but not brown. Stir in the oregano and cumin; cook for 1 minute more.

Add the reserved tomato liquid, tomato sauce, and beer to the onion mixture, and bring to a boil. Reduce the heat and simmer, uncovered, for 10 minutes.

Coarsely chop the reserved stewed tomatoes. Add the tomatoes, black beans, corn, and black pepper to the onion mixture. Simmer, uncovered, until most of the liquid is absorbed and the mixture thickens, about 15 to 20 minutes.

Meanwhile, preheat oven to 400° F. Remove the polenta from the pan, and slice it into 4 squares. Slice each square in half diagonally. Place the polenta on an oiled baking dish, and bake until heated through, about 10 to 12 minutes.

Cut the cooled polenta into 4 squares, then cut the squares diagonally into triangles. To serve, place 2 polenta triangles on a plate. Spoon the chili over the polenta, and top with goat cheese and cilantro, if desired. Enjoy!

Per serving: Calories 368, Protein 11 g, Fat 5 g, Carbohydrates 65 g

1 medium yellow onion, chopped

1 green bell pepper, diced

3 tomatoes, chopped

½ cup chopped fresh pineapple or unsweetened canned pineapple chunks

1 cup chicken-style textured soy chunks*

1 (6-ounce) can tomato paste

1 (4-ounce) can chopped mild green chiles

1 tablespoon blended chili powder

1 teaspoon ground cumin

1 cup cooked black beans

1 cup cooked baby lima beans

Juice of 2 limes

Vegetable stock, to cover

Salt and pepper, to taste

1 tablespoon shredded unsweetened coconut

Sour cream, lime zest, and minced fresh cilantro, for garnish

HAWAIIAN CHILI

Yield: 4 servings

Sweet and hot, like a tropical breeze on the islands, perhaps. Serve this over rice or with lots of tortilla chips.

Combine all of the ingredients, except the coconut and garnishes, in a large pot or Dutch oven, and bring to a boil. Reduce the heat to a simmer, and cook, uncovered, 25 to 30 minutes, stirring often.

Garnish with sour cream, zest, and cilantro, if desired. Enjoy!

* You may substitute 1 cup unflavored textured soy chunks + 1 tablespoon vegetarian "chicken" broth powder for the chicken-style textured soy chunks.

Per serving: Calories 307, Protein 19 g, Fat 3 g, Carbohydrates 49 g

ETHIOPIAN CHILI

Yield: 4 servings

Chiles are a staple food in Northern Africa as they are in any hot climate and combine quite well in the stews and soups of that part of the world. This recipe, then, is not so very far removed from the stews or chilis of the Southwest and Mexico; it boasts just a few different and tasty ingredients. Serve over rice or with hot pita bread.

Combine all of the ingredients, except the cilantro and garnishes, in a large pot or Dutch oven. Cover and bring to a boil. Reduce the heat to a low simmer, and cook, uncovered, 40 to 60 minutes, stirring often. If it becomes too dry, add more water or stock.

Add the cilantro just before serving. Garnish with scallions, tomatoes, and olives, if desired. Enjoy!

Per serving: Calories 478, Protein 14 g, Fat 4 g, Carbohydrates 96 g

1 large sweet potato, peeled and cubed

2 carrots, chopped

1 large white onion, chopped

1 cup millet

2 dried serrano chiles, crushed

½ cup raisins

½ teaspoon ground cumin

½ teaspoon curry powder

2 cups cooked garbanzo beans

Vegetable stock or water, to cover

Salt and pepper, to taste

¼ cup minced fresh cilantro

Chopped scallions, chopped tomatoes, and black olives, for garnish

1 cup chopped fresh basil

8 to 10 cloves garlic, minced

½ cup pine nuts or walnuts

⅓ cup plus 1 tablespoon olive oil

1 medium yellow onion, chopped

4 tomatoes, chopped

2 cups cooked black beans

1 dried serrano chile, crushed

Vegetable juice (such as V-8), to cover

Salt and pepper, to taste

½ cup sour cream (optional)

1 pound pasta, cooked al dente

Grated Parmesan, Asiago, or feta cheese, for garnish

PESTO CHILI

Yield: 4 servings

A very interesting combination of flavors— not quite Italian, not quite Mexican, but definitely quite delicious.

Combine the basil, garlic, and pine nuts or walnuts in a blender or food processor with ⅓ cup of the oil. Process until very smooth.

In a large pot or Dutch oven, sauté the onion and tomatoes in the remaining tablespoon of olive oil over medium-high heat until the onions are tender, about 2 to 3 minutes. Add all of the remaining ingredients, except the sour cream, pasta, and garnishes, adding only enough vegetable juice to keep the stew thick and chunky.

Reduce the heat to a simmer, and cook 20 minutes, adding more vegetable juice, if necessary, if the chili becomes too thick. Mix in the sour cream if desired.

Serve over the pasta and garnish with cheese, if desired. Enjoy!

Per serving: Calories 620, Protein 18 g, Fat 28 g, Carbohydrates 70 g

RAT-A-TAT CHILI

Yield: 4 servings

Sort of a rattatouille with a Mexican accent, this thick stew is delicious over rice. If you'd like to add beans, black beans would go nicely. Or for a deliciously different taste, try fava beans.

Heat the oil in a large pot or Dutch oven, and add the onion, eggplants, zucchini, tomatoes, bell peppers, chiles, and garlic. Sauté for 5 to 10 minutes. When the vegetables are tender, add all of the remaining ingredients, except the rice and garnishes; cover and bring to a low boil.

Remove the cover, reduce the heat to a simmer, and cook for 30 minutes.

Serve over the cooked rice. Garnish with parsley and cilantro, if desired. Enjoy!

2 tablespoons olive oil

1 medium yellow onion, chopped

1 large or 2 small eggplants, diced

2 small zucchini, diced

6 tomatoes, chopped

1 green and 1 red bell pepper, chopped

2 fresh Anaheim chiles, roasted, peeled, and minced

3 cloves garlic, minced

1 teaspoon blended chili powder

1 teaspoon Hungarian paprika

1 teaspoon dried basil or 1 tablespoon minced fresh basil

Vegetable stock, to cover

Salt and pepper, to taste

4 cups cooked brown rice

Minced fresh parsley and minced fresh cilantro, for garnish

Per serving: Calories 384, Protein 8 g, Fat 7 g, Carbohydrates 70 g

2 cups beef-style textured soy granules, or 2 cups unflavored soy granules + ¼ cup tamari or soy sauce

3 unpeeled potatoes, chopped

2 carrots, chopped

1 large white onion, chopped

4 tomatoes, chopped

2 stalks celery, chopped

3 cloves garlic, minced

2 cups tomato sauce

2 cups cooked lima beans

1 teaspoon dried oregano

2 bay leaves

1 teaspoon tamari or soy sauce

Salt and pepper, to taste

Tabasco sauce, to taste

½ cup olive oil

½ cup whole wheat pastry flour

¼ cup Hungarian paprika

Vegetable stock, to cover + 1 cup

Minced parsley, for garnish

HUNGARIAN GOULASH CHILI

Yield: 6 servings

The paprika used traditionally in Hungarian ghoulash is a very tasty but mild variety of chile. Add other peppers if you like. This rich stew is delicious with dark bread and steamed greens. Or try it over rice or pasta.

Combine all of the ingredients except the oil, flour, paprika, and 1 cup of the stock in a large pot or Dutch oven. Bring to a boil and reduce the heat to medium. Cook, stirring often, until the vegetables are tender and the chunks are hydrated, about 20 to 25 minutes.

Meanwhile, in a medium saucepan, heat the oil over medium-high heat. Add the flour and, stirring constantly with a fork or a whisk, combine the flour with the oil and brown lightly. Add the paprika and cook 1 minute more, stirring constantly. Add 1 cup of the vegetable stock a little at a time, still stirring, to make a thick paste or roux.

Add the roux to the chili, and cook, stirring, until it thickens and bubbles. Garnish with parsley, if desired. Enjoy!

Per serving: Calories 477, Protein 21 g, Fat 18 g, Carbohydrates 55 g

BeeT-SOUR CReAM CHiLi

Yield: 4 servings

This is another one I stumbled on by accident. I had leftover beets and leftover chili so, naturally, I mixed the two together—it was delicious.

Combine all of the ingredients, except the cilantro and sour cream, in a large pot or Dutch oven. Cover and bring to a boil over medium-high heat. Uncover, reduce the heat to a simmer, and cook for 35 minutes, stirring frequently.

Top with the sour cream and minced cilantro. Enjoy!

1 medium yellow onion, chopped

1 carrot, diced

1 medium or 2 small beets, diced

4 tomatoes, chopped

2 to 3 cloves garlic, finely minced

1 cup tomato sauce

2 teaspoons blended chili powder

2 dried chilepequin chiles, crushed

2 cups cooked black beans

Vegetable stock or water, to cover

Salt, to taste

1 cup sour cream

1/3 cup minced fresh cilantro

Per serving: Calories 295, Protein 10 g, Fat 10 g, Carbohydrates 39 g

2 tablespoons olive oil

¼ cup red wine

1 teaspoon balsamic vinegar

1 large red onion, chopped

2 green bell peppers, diced

½ pound button mushrooms, sliced

4 tomatoes, chopped

3 cloves garlic, minced

2 fresh jalapeño chiles, roasted, peeled, and minced

1 (3-ounce) can sliced black olives

1 (15-ounce) can plum tomatoes

½ teaspoon blended chili powder

2 bay leaves

Pinch crushed red pepper flakes

MEDITERRANEAN CHILI

Yield: 4 servings

A nice blend of flavors not normally combined in the same dish, this rich stew marries the herbs and flavors of the Mediterranean with the passion and spices of Mexico and Spain. Delightful served with crusty French bread or spooned over rice or pasta!

Combine the oil, wine, and vinegar together in a large pot or Dutch oven. Add the onion and sauté over medium heat for 3 to 5 minutes, stirring frequently. Add the bell peppers, mushrooms, and fresh tomatoes, and sauté for 5 minutes.

Add the garlic, chiles, olives, and canned tomatoes, and sauté for 3 minutes.

Add all of the remaining ingredients, except the fresh herbs and garnishes. Cover and bring to a slow boil. Uncover, reduce heat to a simmer, and cook for 30 minutes.

Before serving, sprinkle with the basil, oregano, and cilantro, and top with cheese, if desired. Enjoy!

1 cup cooked garbanzo beans

1 cup cooked cannellini beans

Vegetable stock, to cover

Salt and pepper, to taste

2 tablespoons minced fresh basil

2 tablespoons each: minced fresh oregano and cilantro

Crumbled feta or Asiago cheese, for garnish

Per serving: Calories 310, Protein 9 g, Fat 12 g, Carbohydrates 38 g

NUCLEAR MELT-DOWN CHILI

NUCLEAR MELTDOWN CHILI

Yield: servings for 4 brave souls

Caution: This spicy hot chili is not for the weak of heart! To soften the blow a little, omit the habañeros; they're extremely powerful.

In a large pot or Dutch oven, heat the oil over medium-high heat. Add the onion and sauté, stirring often, for 3 to 5 minutes. Add the bell pepper and tomatoes, and sauté for 2 to 3 minutes. Add the garlic and sauté 1 minute more.

Add all of the remaining ingredients, except the garnishes, and bring to a slow boil. Reduce the heat to a simmer, and cook for 40 minutes.

Garnish with sour cream, cheese, and cilantro, if desired. Enjoy!

Note: Dairy products can extinguish the blaze that chiles leave in your mouth, so have plenty of them available when you serve up these especially incendiary chilis.

Per serving: Calories 361, Protein 20 g, Fat 7 g, Carbohydrates 52 g

2 tablespoons olive oil

1 large yellow onion, chopped

1 red or green bell pepper, diced

6 tomatoes, chopped

3 cloves garlic, minced

1 cup beef-style textured soy granules, or 1 cup unflavored textured soy granules + 2 tablespoons tamari or soy sauce

1 (6-ounce) can tomato paste

1 tablespoon blended chili powder

1 teaspoon ground cumin

Pinch each crushed and dried habañero, chipotle, and ancho chiles

1 cup fresh or frozen corn

2 cups cooked black beans

Vegetable stock, to cover

Salt and pepper, to taste

Sour cream, grated Monterey Jack cheese, and cilantro, for garnish

Ingredient Sources

Here are sources for some of the ingredients called for in this book, especially beans, chiles, and seasonings. Also, check your local health food store, co-op, Mexican or Asian market, etc.

You never know where you might find just the ingredient you're looking for. One of my favorite sources of salsas and hot sauces is a "99-cent Bargain Store" near my home. They even call me when their shipments of "gourmet foods" (i.e., organic/health food items) come in.

Also, check the Internet. You'd be surprised how a simple "search" for beans or chiles will give you lots of things to check out!

*Many types and flavors of textured soy protein and other meat substitutes; nutritional yeast
Well worth checking out, especially for vegetarians who miss a chewy texture in their dishes.*

A large number of veggie foods, meat substitutes

THE MAIL ORDER CATALOG
P.O. Box 180
Summertown, TN 38483
(800) 695-2241
Fax: (931) 964-2291
catalog@usit.net
www.healthy-eating.com

LUMEN FOODS
409 Scott St.
Lake Charles, LA 70601
(800) 256-2253
Fax: (318)436-1769
support@soybean.com
www.soybean.com

INFINET COMMUNICATIONS, INC.
8551 Cottonwood Road
Bozeman, MT 59718
(406) 585-9324
Fax: (406) 585-0671
or e-mail Rodney at mtmarket@mcn.net

Wheat, barley and a wide variety of beans, many organic, in bulk and at reasonable prices.

Mark Beagle
SUNBIRD PRODUCTS
P.O. Box 2353, Durban, 4000, South Africa
Tel: +27 31 257-455
Fax: +27 31 251-970
sunbird@iafrica.com

A very wide variety of exotic beans and grains.

UNDER THE SUN NATURAL FOODS
1075 Winchester Road
P.O. Box 77
Shady Valley, TN 37688-0077.
(423) 739-9266

A good source of bulk organic beans and textured soy protein. Good prices.

INDIAN HARVEST SPECIALTIFOODS, INC.
P.O. Box 428
Bemidji, MN 56619-0428
(800) 294-2433
www.indianharvest.com

Excellent source of heirloom beans and grains.

SEEDS BLUM
HC 33 BOX 2057
BOISE, ID 83706
(800)-528-3658
Customer Service: (800)-742-1423
Fax: (208)-338-5658

Good source of heirloom beans and seeds.

CHILIS!

Great source of hot sauces and chile products.

MO HOTTA, MO BETTA
P.O. Box 4136
San Luis Obispo, CA 93403
Phone in the USA: (800) 462-3220
Phone Internationally: (805) 544-4051
Fax: (800) 618-4454 or (805) 545-8389
mohotta@mohotta.com
www.mohotta.com

Good source of Hatch (New Mexican) chiles.

SUPERBLY SOUTHWESTERN
2400 Rio Grande Blvd. NW
Box 1-171
Albuquerque, NM 87104-3222
Tel (505) 766-9598
(800) 467-4HOT

Another good source of hatch chiles and edible ristras (chile strings)

HATCH CHILE EXPRESS
P.O. Box 350 -622 Franklin
Hatch, NM 87937
(800) 292-4454 or
Fax: (505) 267-0305.
Phone: (505) 267-3226

My favorite source of posole, native heirloom beans and seeds, dried chiles and powders. A wonderful company to support.

NATIVE SEEDS/SEARCH
526 N. 4th Ave.
Tucson, AZ 85705
(520) 622-5561
Fax: (520) 622-5591
http://desert.net/seeds/home.htm.
nss@azstarnet.com

INDEX

A

Acorn Squash Chili 88
Amaranth Chili 85
Apricot Chili, Savory 101
Artichoke Chili 96
Autumn Harvest Chili 86

B

Barley Chili, Hearty 92
beans
    about 28
    cooking 28-30
    specialty and heritage 36, 123-24
    varieties 31-36
Beet-Sour Cream Chili 117
Black Bean and Corn Chili with Polenta
    110-111
Bulgur-Corn Chili 79
Butter Bean Chili, Midwestern 89
buying chiles 23-24

C

Cactus Chili 67
Calabacitas Chili 64
California Chili 97
Camper's Chili 52

Cape Cod Cranberry-Tofu Chili 100
Caribbean Chili 107
chile powder, about 27
chiles
    as diet food 27
    buying 23-24
    chili and chilies, defined 8
    cooking with 25
    drying 22-23
    eating experience 9-11
    freezing 25
    growing 21-22
    health benefits 13-14
    "high" 14-17
    putting out the fire 26-27
    relative heat levels 18-20
    removing seeds 25
    roasting and peeling 24
    throughout history 11-13
Chili Mac 53
Chili Mac, Tex-Mex 69
Chili Mole 72
chilis, defined 11
condiments and packaged ingredients
    38-40
Corn and Black Bean Chili with Polenta
    110-111
Corn-Bulgur Chili 79
Coyote Chili 61
Cranberry-Tofu Chili, Cape Cod 100

D

drying chiles 22-23

E

Easy Five-Minute Chili 55
Ethiopian Chili 113

F

Five-Bean Chili 56
Four Corners Chili 62
freezing chiles 25

G

Georgia Sweet Potato Chili 104
glossary 46
grains, nuts, and seeds 37-38
Green Chile Stew 71
Greenhouse Chili 65
growing chilies 21-22

H

Hawaiian Chili 112
heat index, defined 16-17
herbs, spices, and seasonings 41-43

I

ingredient sources 122-124

J

Juan's Chili 70

L

Lentil Chili 87

M

Macrobiotic Chili 95
Mango Chili 81
Mediterranean Chili 118
Mexican ingredients 45
Mole Chili 72
Mole, Peanut Chili 102
Mushroom Chile (Three) with Sour
    Cherries 98

N

Nuclear Meltdown Chili 121
nuts, seeds, and grains 37-38

O

oils 40-41

P

Pacifico Chili 68
packaged ingredients and condiments
    38-40
Peanut Chili Mole 102
peeling chiles 24
Pesto Chili 114
Polenta with Black Bean and Corn Chili
    110-111

Portabella and Shiitake Mushroom Chili 109
Posole Chili 66
Potato Chili 63

R

Rat-a-tat Chili 115
Roasted Vegetable Chili 90-91
roasting and peeling chiles 24

S

Scoville units, defined 17
Sedona Redeye Chili 74
seeds, grains, and nuts 37-38
Seitan Chili 83
Shiitake and Portabella Mushroom Chili 109
Sour Cherries, Three-Mushroom Chile with 98
Sour Cream Chili, Beet- 117
Soybean Chili 58
spices, herbs, and seasonings 41-43
Spicy Autumn Harvest Chili 86

Squash Chili, Acorn 88
Sun-Dried Tomato Chili 80
Sweet Potato Chili, Georgia 104

T

Tempeh Chili 84
Tex-Mex Chili Mac 69
Texas White Chili 73
Thai Chili 108
Three-Mushroom Chile with Sour Cherries 98
Tofu Chili 82
Tofu-Cape Cod Cranberry Chili 100
Trucker's Chili, Hearty 54

V

Vegetable Chili, Roasted 90-91
vegetables, in chili 43-44
Vegetarian Chili, Basic 51

W

White Chili, Texas 73

Look for these other fine cookbooks at your favorite bookstore or you can order from:

Book Publishing Co.
P.O. Box 99
Summertown, TN 38483
800-695-2241 http://bpc.thefarm.org

Please add $2.50 shipping per book.

FLAVORS OF THE SOUTHWEST
Robert Oser
$12.95

FABULOUS BEANS
Barb Bloomfield
$12.95

TOFU & SOYFOODS COOKERY
Peter Golbitz
$12.95

TOFU COOKERY
Louise Hagler
$15.95

TOFU QUICK & EASY
Louise Hagler
$9.95

SOYFOODS COOKERY
Louise Hagler
$9.95